Trance by Appointment

Trance by Appointment

Gertrude Trevelyan

Introduction by Louisa Treger
Afterword by Rebecca Bowler

RECOVERED BOOKS
BOILER HOUSE PRESS

Contents

3
Introduction
by Louisa Treger

9
Trance by Appointment
by Gertrude Trevelyan

211
Afterword
by Rebecca Bowler

Introduction

by Louisa Treger

Gertrude Eileen Trevelyan shot to prominence as the first woman to win the Newdigate Prize for poetry at Oxford University in 1927, a feat that became headline news from the US to Australia, and led the *Daily Mail* to declare that her future work "will be watched with interest." She went on to write eight experimental novels, with the *Spectator* hailing her as "an artist [whose] novels have always the fascination of a brilliant technique." She died in 1941 from injuries received during the Blitz and, despite the *Daily Mail*'s prediction, her entire oeuvre lapsed into obscurity.

Trance by Appointment, first published by Harrap in 1939, is Trevelyan's final work. Set in 1930s London it tells the story of Jean, who comes from a working-class family and has psychic powers. Her mother warns: "It's a precious gift to them that can keep their tongue still, but no good ever come to them that didn't. You keep it quiet, my dearie, to yourself." Jean finds a job selling cigarettes from a kiosk in the local Underground station. But the continual ringing of bells, the crashing doors and psychic emanations of the hurrying crowds prove too much for her, and she passes out. Next she works for Madame Eva, a fortune teller, who lives in Bayswater and wants "a nice, quiet, refined sort of girl to 'elp her in the house and learn the business."

At first Jean is happy, feeling "as if she'd found herself." Eva is kind and maternal, and passes on the tricks of her trade: how to sum up her clients by their age, class, and marital status in order to fake clairvoyance and earn her fee. "Always watch their faces... you can tell a lot from faces if you look."

Eva recognises Jean's ability to go into a trance and see visions. "You've got it all right ... you don't want any teaching, you've got it now, got it right inside your 'ead." She discusses Jean with her astrologer friend, Professor Norman Mitch, with his oiled hair brushed across his balding pate and a way of looking at Jean that signals to the reader, if not to Jean, that he is not to be trusted. Before long, Norman has persuaded her to marry him, and he sets her up in a 'Trance by Appointment' business, giving seances and private readings in a West End studio. He persuades her that the visions are transmissions from the dead and that his sweet, deceased sister, Daisy, is her spirit guide. Soon, Jean hears Daisy speaking to her: "Jee-een, I want to talk now."

All goes well until Jean falls pregnant, twice. Norman blames her, as if he bears no responsibility for her condition. Childbirth and exhaustion disrupt the seances, and he takes his anger out on her. What follows is a pitch-perfect evocation of a coercive, controlling relationship. Periodically, Norman abandons Jean. We watch her children grow. Their son turns out badly because Norman alternately indulges and beats him. Their daughter is terrified of her father and Jean soon realises why: she has inherited her clairvoyance.

The narrative is interwoven with excerpts from the lives of other mediums; slovenly, impatient, greedy women who are clearly fakes. They act as a foil for Jean, emphasising both the sincerity and the rarity of her gifts. Ironically, by the end of the novel, Jean has become one of them; exploiting her clients for financial gain in order to save enough money to stop her daughter being exploited by Norman, as she was.

Despite the colloquial tone, the overwhelming atmosphere is one of claustrophobia. Jean has few choices in her life, and almost no will. Why doesn't she leave Norman? She could go back to her parents, or start up her own psychic business, but she never does. The narrative moves from third person to first person and back again, between inner and outer worlds in a way that is reminiscent of Virginia Woolf or Dorothy Richardson. However, there is nothing free flowing or poetic about Jean's consciousness. Her thoughts are expressed in brief, repetitious sentences, as though the language is as trapped as she is. "'Daisy duck, you will help me though, won't you,' she stated, laying out the cards. 'You will, won't you, Daisy. Daisy love, I haven't ever needed it so much.'"

The effect is mesmerising. The gradual wearing down of Jean carries the tension of a thriller. We almost can't bear to read on and yet we can't stop reading. Somehow—and the reader can't quite work out how she does it—Trevelyan's depiction of this small, constricted life is utterly gripping. *Trance by Appointment* is a powerful, thought-provoking book that stays with the reader long after they have read the final page, leaving them troubled and uncertain.

Why, then, has Trevelyan's work been forgotten? No doubt she suffered from the centuries-old bias that meant women were dismissed as domestic rather than being taken seriously as authors. She was financially independent and had a room in Notting Hill—prerequisites for being able to write well, according to Virginia Woolf in *A Room of One's Own* (1929). This meant that she spent her days experimenting with the style and structure of the novel—she did not need to teach, review, edit or otherwise participate in the literary life of the day, so she did not have the same opportunity to integrate with her peers, people who might have helped to keep her legacy alive.

Whatever the reason for her obscurity, it is cause for rejoicing that Boiler House Press is bringing out new editions of her best novels. Her work is still relevant and topical, given that we are yet again grappling with big questions about controlling relationships, what women are told we must believe about ourselves, and the struggle to have our stories heard and understood on our own terms. Trevelyan's work remains an important part of the literary canon and can now be appreciated by a new audience.

Trance by Appointment

by Gertrude Trevelyan

To Julia

I

Joyce backed the mailcart up against the hoarding and kicked a stone under the wheel, "Be good girl now, Jee-een." She lifted Jean up and pushed her back, further in, between the wooden sides of the mailcart, and tightened up the strap across her tummy; her face was all pursed up and busy like Mum's. "Back presen'ly, bye-bye." She was running off down to the corner to play, where Ted and the others were calling out.

Jean sat and gurgled, with the strap across her tummy. She gurgled up at the big coloured lady on the hoarding, but it was too high up to reach. There was a paper running along the pavement, it went flap-flap and ran along and stopped, and flapped and ran along again and turned over. Jean gurgled and bumped up and down on the seat, and the back went bump-bump against the hoarding. And there was a boy on a bicycle, he bumped up and down and whistled, and the bicycle went squiggly, one way and then the other, all along the road.

And then there was a big blue bubble and it burst, and another, and white ones too, big and shiny, and Jean gurgled and grabbed at them, but they went away, and then there were more. And when she shut her eyes up tight the bubbles were bigger and brighter, and they jumped about, and Jean gurgled and bumped up and down.

Then she got sleepy and wriggled round till her face was lying on the wood back, but it was hard. So she wriggled down further, with her head against her shoulder, and went to sleep.

Then it jogged and she woke up, and Joyce got down and sat her up again, "Come on Jee-een, going home now," and Ted was turning round on his roller-skate out in the road, making a big rattle. Joyce went behind and pushed Jean, and they went bump-bump along the pavement, and Norah was walking alongside, rubbing her nose with the back of her hand; when Jean was sat up on the seat she was as tall as Norah. They stopped at the shop on the corner and Joyce sent Norah in for the butter Mum said to get, and when she came out with it in a paper bag Joyce pushed it down on the seat alongside Jean. And then she called out after Ted who was skating right down the middle of the road, push-ing with his other foot, "Te-ed! Come on! You won't 'arf catch it if Mum sees you!"

Jean woke and it was dark, it wasn't day yet. She turned over on her back and wriggled away from Norah's elbow that was stick-ing out and bumped into Joyce, Joyce made a noise and turned over. Jean lay still on her back between Joyce and Norah and held her breath so that they didn't wake up, and looked at the dark, because if you kept still and looked hard the bubbles would come and things, more than in the daytime. There was a big river with little boats on, like the canal where Tom went fishing tiddlers, and trees all along instead of houses. And if you went on and on, where it turned round....

She opened her eyes wide and hugged the sheet, and then it

was getting light and there wasn't any more. There was the black rail at the bottom of the bed, and the washstand; and Norah made a black lump under the clothes, with the window at the back of her and the bar across under the blind. Joyce turned over and said sleepily, "What is it, Jee-een," and threw an arm round. Jean snuggled down and went to sleep again.

Mum was getting the dinner and Jean was helping and the others weren't home from school yet. Dad was back, he was reading his paper. His feet took up a lot of room and Jean had to go round every time and when she fell over he didn't look. Mum was peeling the potatoes up on the table and when a bit of peel fell on the floor Jean picked it up and carried it round Dad's feet and round past the dresser and over the floor of the back kitchen that was all ups and downs, and put it in the ash-bucket. And then she came back over the floor and round the dresser and over Dad's feet to see if there was any more down. It was rough and hard on one side and white and smooth and wet on the other and you could twist it into shapes. Jean sat down on the floor and twisted a long squiggly peel round her fingers, and all the time she was talking hard but they didn't take any notice. "And it was a great big boat going on and on all twiggly round the corners, and it was all full up with people, and when it got to the corner it went bump and they all fell down." She squiggled the peel round and round and then it broke. "Where does it come from, Mum?"

"What, lovey?"

"The trees and things that come when it's dark. When you lie and look hard, but you have to keep still as still or it goes. And the bubbles that's all different colours and jumps about, where does it come from, Mum?"

"Stuff and nonsense. Is my water boiling yet?"

It was going pop-pop under the cover. Mum got up and put the potatoes in.

"But there is, they do. And when you shut your eyes tight, but most in the dark. There was all great big trees upstairs last night, and a great big river with fishes an' boats in."

"Don't tell lies," said Dad. His hand in his shirt-sleeve brought the paper down lower so he could look over the top. There were funny hairs on his wrist and a bit of cotton hanging from his cuff. Then he pulled the paper up again.

"There *was*, reely-truly."

"Get along with you," Mum said.

Then there was Auntie Lil there and Mum. Auntie Lil was fat and pretty and her frock smelt of violets. And she had acid drops in her bag, that stuck to the lining and if you pulled you could get them off.

Mum was telling Auntie Lil, "It's the second sight, the same Granny Jenkins 'ad."

Auntie Lil said, "I never 'ad it."

"Well I did," said Mum. "I used to. But you lose it when you get older."

Auntie Lil said, "Jean lovey, come over 'ere and tell Auntie Lil what you can see."

Jean wriggled round with her back to them. "Don't see nothing." She went on digging for acid-drops in Auntie Lil's bag, where it was all funny and smelly and powdery and made you sneeze.

"She's shy," Mum said. "Come here, lovey. Tell Auntie Lil about the big boat that was upstairs, there's a good girlie."

"I know a little girl likes sweeties," said Auntie Lil. "I wonder if Jeannie doesn't like sweeties. I got a whole packet of them here in my pocket."

Jean wriggled round, but they weren't looking anymore.

"Let me give you another cup," Mum said, and she and Auntie Lil went on talking.

Presently Auntie Lil turned round. "Why, here's Jeannie come to see Auntie Lil! What do you want then, duckie?"

"Want sweeties."

"Please," said Mum.

"Let her alone," said Auntie Lil. "Now lovey, you shall 'ave your sweeties. You just look 'ard at Auntie Lil and shut your eyes tight and tell 'er what you see."

Jean shut her eyes tighter and tighter until the colours began to come, and then she jumped about with her eyes shut tight. "Oo, it's all lovely colours! And flowers, like vilets. All growing in big bunches. And... and... That's all!"

She opened her eyes and it was all going round, and Auntie Lil caught her on her lap.

"There now! Just fancy! And a little bit of a thing like that!"

Then she felt in her pocket. "There, there's your sweeties, lovey."

Then there was Auntie Lil again, that was another time. She and Mum were having their tea, and Auntie Lil said, "She *is* getting a big girl. What are you going to do with 'er? You ought to put 'er to telling fortunes at the fair when she's grown, didn't you?"

But Mum went cross. "I don't hold with that, as you very well know. That's all lies. Those that 'ave the Sight keep it to themselves."

"Can't I go to the fair, Mum?"

Mum jumped, and she and Auntie Lil both laughed. "There isn't any fair, my duckie. You run along and see if Joyce and them aren't coming from school."

"But, Mum, Auntie Lil just said...."

"There, there's a penny to spend. Now run along, and don't cross over the road, mind."

Jean jumped along from square to square along the pavement, with the penny getting hot in her hand, she held it so tight. What was that Auntie Lil said then, about the fair coming? There hadn't been a fair come to Edenfields since she was big enough, only the circus, and it was a bit like that, Joyce said, Joyce and Ted went to the fair once. Coo, she'd like to go!

And then, just while she was hopping along, three squares on one foot and three on the other, there was the fair coming, just there, away up at the end of the road! No not reely-truly, it was one of *them*. She shut her eyes tight and saw it clear as clear—a lovely lady on a horse, just like in the circus, and elephants, and a funny-man with a tall hat. Then she jumped on a stone and opened her eyes and it wasn't there anymore. And then there were the others, coming from school.

"I got a penny to spend! And I saw the fair! There's a fair coming, I saw it!"

"Go on, you never did." Ted was skating past on his roller-skate, he made a sweep round and came back. "You never did then. Fair's only coming Monday week, bank 'oliday."

Norah came jumping up. "'Ave you got a penny Jean, ree-ly-truly? Where d'you get it from? What you going to get?"

"Mum give it me. To get sweeties. Yes, I did see the fair then."

"Go on, you didn't."

"Yes, I did."

Joyce bent down and took her hand. "Come along, duckie, come to the shop. Do leave her Ted, why shouldn't she see it?"

"'Tisn't 'ere yet, that's why."

"There was a lovely lady all on a horse like in the circus, and a funny-man in a 'at, and...."

"Go on, you saw the posters up. There's one down by home."

"No I didn't, I saw it inside."

"Never mind, duckie. Now what you want to buy? Tell Joyce."

"Licrice drops."

Jean had hold of Joyce's hand. Joyce had the threepence each to go in that Mum gave her and a penny to spend all round. There was Joyce and Ted and Norah and Jean, but Ted went off after the big boys from school that were standing round outside whistling through their fingers, and then he came back and came up to

Joyce, "'Ere, you give me my lot, come on."

"Woffor? We all got to pay to go in."

"Go on, you aren't going to pay a whole threepence just for going in. All the chaps don't, they gets in under the canvas, round the back."

"Te-ed, you naughty boy! You'll get found out, you will!"

He got his fourpence off her and she sent him a clip over the ear. But he was off, catching up with the others, running round the outside of the bumpy canvas wall that was put up all round the fairground.

Joyce took hold of Jean's hand and pushed Norah in front and they went in through the turnstile between the tents, where the grass was all trodden down by the people walking. It was lovely inside, you could hear the music louder and louder. There was a roundabout with horses and ostriches going round slow with nobody on it, with the man shouting to come and have a ride.

"Can we 'ave a ride, Joyce?"

"Later on, duckie. There isn't many here yet, we're early."

She took Norah's hand on the other side and they walked round over the tumpy grass where there were the tents up saying, "Walk Inside, World's Greatest Living Wonder," and the shooting galleries, and swings that were going slow waiting for you to get in. There was a boy in one, going up ever so high.

They stopped to watch a lady throw at the hoop-la, and then Joyce said "'Ullo," and Lucy Smiff said "'Ullo!" It was Lucy Smiff had come up, and she took Joyce's other arm that Norah had let go of, and hung on. "Come on, let's walk round."

They started off over the grass among the people that were coming in, with Joyce holding on to Jean's hand; and Jean kept pulling back, she wanted to see if the lady was going to get anything at the hoop-la.

Joyce said, "Come on, Jee-een," and pulled, and Jean had to catch up; she had to run nearly, Joyce and Lucy were walking so fast, and laughing with their heads together. There were a lot of people now and they got in the way, and when they got in between Joyce kept tugging at Jean's arm to make her come round.

Then there was Norah, who'd gone with some of the others, Etty Stokes and them, they were over buying ginger-snaps from a man had got them on a tray.

Just then Joyce and Lucy stopped by the coconut-shies and Lucy took a pennyworth and Joyce let go to watch, and Jean started off to Norah, all among the people. She fell down once, and it was all muddy, but when she got up she'd got there nearly. They'd got the ginger-snap in a newspaper cornet, and were sharing it round, saying where they'd go next.

"Wadjer want? Awright, come on." They put a bit in her mouth and it was sticky and hard and went crunch when you bit, and then they started on round the tents with Jean keeping up.

Etty Stokes was the daring one. The others dared her to get down behind a tent and look in under, where you could hear them clapping, and she did, and she said, "Oo it's lovely, it's where they're haying the the-ater!" So they all got down and looked, but you couldn't see anything but the people's feet, so they all went on to the next.

Then Jean fell over a rope that was stuck out holding up a tent, and fell down in the mud. The others were going on and she called out, "Wait for me-ee!"

One of them jogged Norah, "There's your Jean fell down." So Norah came back and picked her up, her frock was all muddy down the front, and popped a bit of ginger-snap into her mouth. "Go on, go and look for Joyce. Go on." And then she ran off to catch up with the others, but Jean ran on after them.

They got round the back of a tent that was all red and yellow and there was a man stood up in front calling out. Etty Stokes said, "You watch *me*!" and got down with her hands and knees in the mud and looked right in under. "It's the *fortune*-teller!"

Then they all got down and looked, and you couldn't lift up the tent more than a bit, you had to lay down with your head sideways and look like that. And there was a lady sat there having her fortune told, and the fortune-teller was all dressed up in red and black shawls all down over her, you could see her big boots coming out underneath all covered up with mud. And a shawl right over her head and big earrings on like curtain-rings, and you could hear her talking, only you couldn't hear anything because of the big steam roundabout round outside playing tunes all the time, and all the people walking. Etty Stokes was saying, just behind, "Coo, don't I just wish I could 'ave mine told!"

Jean wriggled her head right inside, it was lovely, it wasn't like anything she had ever seen before. It was ever so dark inside and you couldn't see the fortune-teller's face, she was bent right down looking at the lady's hand and the big gold earrings went bob with the way she was nodding at it. Jean wriggled right in till her tummy was flat in the mud, with the tent on her back, and she was lying on her arms on the grass inside the tent where it wasn't trodden down. And then she was frightened all at once and started to wriggle back, only she did want to hear what the fortune-teller was telling the lady so she wriggled back in again.

And then she was getting pulled out from behind, and there was a big man, the one from round in front. "Now then you, you little 'un, you be off, sharp."

She dodged round the tent and fell over a rope and scrambled up quick and ran, in case the man was going to run after, but he only stood and looked. All the others weren't there and it was full of people. She ran in between them and past the roundabouts and fell down again and got up and started to cry, and someone said, "Where's your muvver, little girl?" But she only ran on again, until she tripped over a lady's umbrella and fell down.

Joyce got her by the arm and dragged her up, and she was all over mud down her front and over her knees. Joyce held her up by her arm and gave her a slap on her cheek and shook her and she started crying out loud with her mouth open. "Where you been to? What you want to run away for, you naughty little girl!"

Lucy Smiff was there, she'd got a china clock with pink roses on she won at the hoop-la.

"Come on now. Come on 'ome."

Joyce had her by the hand and she was dragging along with her mouth open, crying.

"Do stop it, Jee-een!"

Lucy had a paper of ginger-snaps, and they stuffed her mouth full to make her stop crying. "Come on now, duckie."

Joyce and Lucy took arms and pushed on through the people, back to the gate, dragging Jean along with them. She was crying with her mouth open, so the tears ran in and tasted all salt along with the ginger-snap.

"Mum, what the fortune-teller does, is it the same as when you see things? Like when you shut your eyes up tight?"

"No, my duckie, fortune-tellers is all lies. Don't you never have nothing to do with them."

"Ted says it's all lies saying you can see things in your head. Doesn't everyone see them, Mum?"

"Only those that has the Sight."

"What's the Sight, Mum?"

"What makes you see what others can't. But don't you go puzzling over it, now. It's a precious gift to them that can keep their tongue still, but no good ever come to them that didn't. You keep it quiet, my dearie, to yourself."

And so she did. She used to try hard to keep awake at nights, long as ever she could, to see pictures when it got dark, and she never nudged the others and said "Look," because you mustn't and they couldn't see anyhow. Only sometimes she went off to sleep before it would come. And she used to hop along the pavement, hugging herself round her middle, because she'd got a secret all to herself and they didn't know.

Only when she got up a big girl and went to school along with the others Norah went and told Etty Stokes, and she told all the rest, "Our Jean comes over queer and sees things."

It was one day they were all out in the yard for play, and some of the big ones that were walking round came up and stopped and started telling her off, "Go on, you can't see nothing?"

And one of them calling out, "Come on then, what's Teacher doin' now?"

Then they all got round, and Jean shut up her eyes tight, but there wasn't anything but blackness.

"Come on little 'un, tell us what Teacher's doin'!"

"Cuddlin' wiv Mr. Jukes!"

Then they all let out a big shout and a laugh and the big ones went off walking round, and the little ones, that had stopped playing tick[1] to listen, started calling out and going on again, and Jean was left standing alone by herself. And then she went in the corner behind the dustbins and cried, because she didn't know whatever made her say that dreadful thing, she only heard herself say it afterwards. Because it was all lies, and if you went telling lies about it you wouldn't see things anymore. And then the bell went, and they had to go back into school.

Jean was a good girl at school. She learned her lessons, and didn't behave silly like some. She used to go to school with Joyce, because Ted would be off on his own and so would Norah by now, off with the others. Joyce was in the top standard, she'd be leaving soon. She used to see Jean had her nose wiped, and tell her to be a good girl and do what she was told, and take her round and leave her

---

1   Children's game also known as tag.

at the "Infants" door, before she went on into "Girls."

By the time Joyce left and went out into service Jean was out of the Infants, in the big school along with Ted and Norah. Ted was in the top standard now, and Norah was in the middle, and Jean was at the bottom. She used to go with Norah sometimes, but Norah and her lot were always larking round and they couldn't be bothered with Jean, she was one of the quiet ones. So she used to go off to school by herself most days, making up stories to herself in her head and sometimes seeing them happen.

When Ted had passed out of the top standard too he went to work at a garage. So then there was only Jean and Norah. Norah wasn't moved up, because she wouldn't learn, she was ever so lazy; and Jean wasn't, she used to work hard and do what anyone told her, so she was moved up among the bigger girls, and now she was only one standard off Norah.

Ted used to come home to dinner these days all over grease from the garage, and Jean used to tell him to go and wash himself, but he only laughed. Mum didn't like it either. One time Auntie Lil was there Mum was telling her about it, how he was got so rough. And then Jean heard her say, "My Jeannie, she's a real little lady."

Jean was ever so pleased. It used to worry her sometimes how she wasn't pretty like Norah. Norah was ever so pretty, with fair, curly hair. None of the rest of them had hair like that, and she used to curl it round her finger in the morning when Jean wanted to get to the glass. "Go on," she used to say, "*you* don't want to look at yourself."

Jean's hair was straight down her back, and it wasn't any colour at all, and she hadn't got pink cheeks like Norah, either. But Mum didn't ever tell Norah she was like a lady, she was too loud. Always larking round, and starting to go after the boys.

And when the new baby came it was Jean had to look after her and bathe her and tie on her bib and take her out in the mailcart after school. Norah was doing up her curls, or gadding off with that Etty Stokes, the bold thing! And Mum couldn't do anything with her.

Dad told her off once. He said he'd give her the strap if he ever saw her going off again with that Etty Stokes and her boys. But Norah didn't care, she only waited till Dad was out at work.

Jean would sit Baby Doris in the mailcart and do up the strap over her tummy and wheel her out along the street to the recreation ground. When they got there she'd back the mailcart up against the wall and kick a stone under the wheel and get down and do the strap up tighter, "Be good girl now, Dor-ris," and then run off and play with Bessie Jetters on the seesaw.

When she had the shopping to do for Mum she'd wheel Doris along up to the shops, and sometimes Bessie would come too, and then when they'd done their shopping and pushed the parcels down on the seat alongside Doris they'd go for a walk over the railway bridge, along by the allotments.

When Norah left school she went to be an usherette at the cinema. Dad said he'd give her what-for if she didn't come straight home after the picture was over. But she didn't care, she used to stay out ever so late, she didn't care for anyone.

Doris was getting a big girl now, but Jean still used to push her in the mailcart when they went out for a walk along with Bessie Jetters. Sometimes they'd let her out to walk a bit, but then she'd start crying and dragging behind and Jean would have to lift her up and strap her back in the cart, "Do shut up, Dor-ris," and slip a sweetie in her mouth to make her stop, "There lovey, be good girl now," and push her on again so they could go on talking.

One day Bessie said, going pink all of a sudden, "I say Jean, tell us, is it true what the girls say about you?"

"What?"

"What they say, that you can tell fortunes? I say Jean, will you tell my fortune for me?"

"Fortunes is all lies," Jean said. "That's what Mum says."

Bessie took hold of the mailcart so that it went jog over a stone and Doris started whimpering—"Do shut up, Dor-ris"—and wheedled round Jean, "Oh go on do, you know you can, can't you Jean, do look at my 'and for me, do, go on."

"I can't see things in 'ands Bessie, I never did. You 'ave to learn 'ow."

"Oh go on, try, go on."

"Oh awright."

They jogged the mailcart down over the grass at the side of the road, where there was the grass all tumpy and dusty between the road and the wires of the allotments. They sat down on the grass with their backs to the road, looking at the cabbages through the wires.

"Come on, do."

Jean picked up Bessie's hand she'd put on her knee, and frowned at it. You could see the lines clear, there was dirt in them, clear as clear. "And it all means something. I do wish I knew it."

"Oh go on, you've only got to look and you can see things. They all said you can."

Jean stared down hard at the dirty lines on Bessie's hand, but they didn't mean anything she knew about. And then she saw it, all at once: "I know what it is, why you want it told, you want to know about Jim Utchins, if 'e's sweet on you like you are on 'im."

"'Owever did you know that?"

"I just saw it."

"No you didn't then, you seen me with 'im."

"I did see you with 'im, but I didn't know you're sweet on 'im."

"'Ow'd you know then? Did you see it there? Go on, tell us."

"I saw it just now. But he isn't on you, though, not like you are on 'im."

"Oh go on, you aren't seeing it right, you're only pretendin' to, aren't you Jean? Go on, say you are."

"No I'm not then, I'm seein' it all clear. Jim Utchins isn't sweet on you, he's sweet on Elsie Parks, there now!"

"Oh go on, the nasty cat!"

"But he won't marry 'er, nor anyone from round 'ere, but someone different. And the same with you."

"No! Who, then? Go on!"

Jean looked round, and she saw Bessie all funny as if she was waking up and seeing her. "I dunno. I didn't see any more."

"Well go on, look some more."

Jean shook her head. "I can't. It's gone." She reached out for Doris and gave the cart a jog.

"Oh go on, you are a mean thing! Why can't you?"

"I dunno. Come on, we got to go 'ome." She got up and pulled Doris up on the road again.

Bessie was mad with her then. "I don't believe you saw any of it. You weren't looking, I saw you. And you don't know 'ow to see it any'ow, you said you didn't."

"Yes I did then. I didn't know I could, but I did. I saw it clear as clear."

"You weren't looking at my 'and at all, so there. And I don't believe in it, what's more."

"Awright, don't then. Come on lovey, going 'ome now."

She tucked in Doris and bent down and pushed hard behind her all the way home along the road. Bessie came along too, she was all red and cross, but she had to come too because there wasn't any other way back.

"You are a mean cat," Bessie said. "I don't believe that about Jim Utchins."

"What d'you go asking for, if you don't want to know."

"And I'm not sweet on 'im anyway, so there."

When they got back under the railway bridge Bessie turned off the way she lived, she didn't even say good-bye. Jean didn't care, she went on pushing Doris along home, along the streets.

She didn't care if Bessie was sweet on Jim Utchins or if she wasn't, and she didn't care if Jim Utchins was sweet on Bessie or who, she knew she'd seen right. She hadn't ever seen it like that before, not when she wanted to. And it wasn't Bessie's hand either, it just came over her, the minute she said, "I know what it is." It all came to her, like that.

When she'd put Doris to bed that night and got in along with her and hugged her up to make her go off, she lay awake and tried to remember the way it came. She mustn't ever let Mum know, Mum would be mad with her, going telling what she saw. She saw it all right though, clear as, as anything, clear as clear. Saw it all right. Don't care what Bessie says. Bessie's a cat. "What is it lovey? Go to sleep, do." A cat, that's what that Bessie is. Don't care for *her*, saw it all right. Yes I did then. Saw it clear as, clear as, clear's clear.

A

"Tell yer fortune, lady? Cross yer palm wiv silver?"

Hoop-la and coconut-shies and mud and fust and brandysnaps. And the MER-ry-go-round goes round. ...Ow, Erbert!

Walk up, walk up, ladies and gentlemen!

Two frows a penny, two frows a penny, two frows a...goes round, goes round....

"An' there's luck comin' to yer from over the sea.

"Thank yer, lady, bless yer, lady.

"Tell yer fortune, lady?"

II

Doris was going in the Infants by the time Jean left school. Jean had to get her up and take her along with her on her way to work, leave her at the gate—"There, lovey, be good now"—and then run back and catch the bus to take her in to High Lanes Tube Station where she was working, selling in the tobacco kiosk.

It was a big new station at High Lanes, and they had ever so many come through at the rush-hours. The Tube didn't go any further, and they used to come in there from all around on the buses. She'd hardly have time to get the shutters down in the mornings and slip inside and pop her bag down on the shelf under the counter before they started coming through. "Small Player's." "Box matches, please, miss." But they hadn't got much time for please, that time of the morning. Slap down their sixpence on the glass tray and snatch up the packet before she could hardly put it down, having to reach up behind for it on the shelves. And the later ones wouldn't stop even for that—sooner go without their fags. There was the bell going for the train to start down below, and the lift-doors banging open, and their hats and white faces all in a hurry pushing past her and in, afraid they'd miss the next, and the doors crashing to and the lift creaking and another bell: and some that had got there too late standing chewing themselves by the empty cage where the lift had gone down. Got up too late for his breakfast, that one. Sick-feeling, down in his stomach. And then the lift up again, and them hurrying in—leaning up against the side, bent down over his paper—though it wouldn't start down yet, not till that train was gone out; and then the bell, down underground, and the lift crashing to, half empty this time, and creaking down till there was only the ropes shaking. That was the lot, except for one or two; the end of all that lot. Till getting on for later in the morning, when the women would start coming through, going up further in for their shopping.

Jean picked up the feather-whisk from under the counter and started to flick the dust off the shelves of tins and packets in their shiny paper wrappings. There was hardly room to turn round inside there, even though she was as thin as a rake, and every now and then as she turned she would put up her elbow and push back a box her arm had jerked out of line, with reaching up and bending down. When she got round again to the counter she wiped over its chromium-plated top and the glass tray for the money and the brightly-coloured boxes of harlequin matches that stood to one side and the orphanage collecting-box with the label half torn off that was pushed back against the other, and slipped the whisk away on the shelf underneath, under the cash-register, and sighed, straightening her back, catching a draggled wisp of hair away behind her ear with her slide.

Once the rush had gone through there was hardly anyone. There was the empty cage of the lift, and the pigeon-hole of the booking-office, empty, just across. The clerk was sat down having a read, you could see the top of his head across the counter. The booking-hall was quite empty and light; you could see right out past the paper-stall to the Parade outside. Sometimes someone would go by on the pavement, or go in one of the shops—the greengrocer's or the post-office-sweet-shop, across the street.

The lift came up lazily and the doors crashed back, the lift-man took a look round the empty hall and strolled over to the booking-office. He stood there, leaning on his elbow, having a chat. The doors of the empty lift stood wide open, you could see the advertisements on the walls inside: Madame Freesia's School of Dancing; Court Hairdressing, 18 The Parade.

A fellow came in from the street; the girl at the Papers gave him a smile—she was one of the fast ones—and he stopped and bought one and stood there with his hat on the back of his head, chaffing with her, she gave a laugh. Then he came on up the hall, not in a hurry, with his paper under his arm, up to the booking-of-fice, and the liftman strolled across, whistling, and took him down.

There were the women coming through later on—not the sort that was in a hurry, going to work like the men, but those that were slow and fussy, fussing with their handbags and their gloves. One of them wanted pipe tobacco for her husband. The trains didn't go so often, mid-morning; now and then there was the bell going down below, and the doors shutting and the lift creaking down; and presently it would come up and the doors bang back. Then there'd be long stretches when the hall was empty to the street and the sun coming in, almost up to the Papers; and you could see that one patting up her waves, getting ready for them coming back through for the dinner-hour.

You could feel it long before they got there, Jean could—almost as if you could hear the trains coming, packed up, all in a hurry, getting home to dinner; and yet you couldn't. You wouldn't have known it till the lift came up full all of a sudden, and they came crowding out past to the street, making no end of a clatter, shutting out the light and air. Not so many as in the morning, and those that did come didn't think of anything but their dinner;

they didn't stop hardly, that lot. And less than an hour later they'd be back through, pick up a packet of fags very likely, quick as she could give it to them, and all gone again, down underground. Then she'd slip round home for her own dinner, while the boy took over, and then back for the afternoon, when there weren't many; but those that did come had time to hang about, chaffing with the one at the Papers.

Once a fellow tried it on with Jean; one of the afternoon ones that didn't know what to do with himself. Asking a large Player's and trying to take her hand along with it. She pulled it off quite rough; she was ever so upset—and she in there not able to get away, nor to turn round hardly. She stood right back, back against the shelves, with such a look at him. And he just gave a snigger and swaggered off; he was only trying it on to see if she was that sort, like that one down there.

And Mum was ever so upset when she heard about it. "And my Jeannie always been so refined."

"Slap 'is face for 'im," Norah called out from upstairs. "That's what you ought to do when they start gettin' fresh." She was always a bold one.

And Auntie Lil was there too. "It isn't the sort of job for 'er, it isn't what you ought to 've put 'er to. You ought to put 'er to some nice, quiet, refined sort of a job."

"There aren't the jobs going," Mum said, worried-looking. "But my Jeannie's always been nice and refined.

They didn't often try it on, though. It was only one or two. Half of them looked right through you as if you weren't there. Mostly they didn't have time to see who it was, even: slap down their money for what they wanted and get on off to work, or else home. And most full of worry and bother of some sort—got their own worries. That was the worst in a way; how they all came through with their worries, and afraid, most of them—afraid they'd be late, or one thing or another; and you couldn't help feeling it.

You'd think going home at night they'd cheer up a bit and take it easier, but that was the worst of the lot. Tired, that was what it was. Made it worse for them. You could tell them coming then all right, getting on for the rush-hour. There wouldn't be any rush-hour yet out at High Lanes, only a few passing in the street, and the one at the Papers patting up her hair; and yet all at once you'd feel it was all a noise and hurry, and so tired out you didn't know what to do; she didn't know how the liftman could stand there so casual knowing he'd have to go down in a minute and have them come crowding in. Then he'd go off down, easy, humming a tune; and in a minute there was the train bell, and the lift up again, heavy, as if it could hardly move, and when the doors were thrown open they pushed out like falling out of something, and filled up right to the street with hats and raincoats and tired-looking faces before you could look round. Jean leaned behind her little counter. "Small Gold Flake." "Box matches, miss." She could hardly reach our fast enough to put them down. But a lot just went by, pushing, with their attaché cases. By the time that lot had gone through and the lift gone down for the next the place was so full of fret and flurry you could hardly breathe.

One day there was a young fellow stopped for a packet of fags, and he was so tired out you couldn't help notice; mostly she didn't even look up at them, didn't trouble half the time, but there was something about this one made her notice him, how white and drawn his face was. Looked as if he hadn't slept for a week. Quite a young chap too. He must have had a bad day at the office. "Thank you, miss," he said, ever so civil and respectful, not like a lot of them.

"Don't mention it," she said. She hardly ever said so much.

She couldn't help feeling sorry for him, the tired way he went off; watching him dodge his way out through the crows, pulling at his shabby old case, in a hurry to get home. Maybe his wife's ill, and he's been fretting all day.

It was a funny thing, he came into her mind again when she was home having her tea. She couldn't help thinking of him getting back after a hard day at the office and having to get his tea for himself very likely, with his wife ill upstairs. Luck thing he hadn't got any children, wasn't it?

Now whatever made her think that? He hadn't ever said so.

She didn't see him again for a day or two, that one; kept busy while the rush was on. But then one morning when he was a bit early and the hall emptier than usual she saw him coming in, stepping out brisk, and not so bothered-looking. She's better to-day, she thought. It made her feel better all day, flicking the dust off the cartons, and leaning, easing her back—she did get the backache something dreadful with all the standing—until they started coming back through again.

And then one dinner-time when he came up to buy something—"Thank you, miss," he said, though he was in a hurry, you could see that—he looked so tired and worried again she couldn't help speaking to him.

"Nasty wet day," she said. "Cold, too."

You could see it out in the street, running wet on the pavements. He ought to put his mack on; got it dragging down over his arm.

He quite jumped. "Yes?" he said. "Wet," he said. "Nasty." He stood a minute holding the packet of fags on the way to his pocket, as if he wondered whether he'd say something more. "Good-day," he said, shy all of a sudden, and pushed the fags into his pocket and slipped off among the crowd, out into the rain, with the mack dragging down over his arm. Can't stop here talking, can he? She mightn't like it.

She used to wonder about him sometimes, that shy one. But there were so many you didn't often get to notice or know any by sight. And most didn't come from round High Lanes, even; used to go and queue up outside for the buses that went on further out. You could see them shiver, these winter nights, coming up out of the life from where it was warm, down below, and getting out in the wet street. It was draughty even here, up at the top of the hall; Jean used to pull her cardigan tight round her shoulders and stand back against the shelves, trying to keep out the draught, when there wasn't anyone.

Her feet would get sopping wet too, getting there in the mornings. She had to take Doris to the school, because Norah wouldn't be up yet—her work didn't start till middle-day—and then go back and stand for the bus.

She got in and took down the shutters, and then the rush started, and by the time it was over her feet were chilled through. She stamped up and down to warm them before she did the dusting round. You'd think that one down at the Papers would die of cold out there by the street, but she didn't seem to feel it, with her low-necked jumpers in all weathers. Got plenty of flesh on her to keep her warm. Norah was always telling Jean off for being so skinny.

The afternoons were the worst, though—after they started coming back, about five o'clock. And especially the later ones—the first were the bosses, they didn't feel it so bad. But getting on for six to half-past it was as if she could feel them coming, long before the lift came up. While the booking-hall was nearly empty, and quietish, in between trains, except for the clerk and the liftman having a chat, and you could see right out in the street where the rain was shining on the lit pavements, out past where the one at the Papers was standing chaffing with a fellow. You could feel all those trains coming packed full—all those fellows so wet and fed-up like; and the long tramp in the rain they'd got ahead of them, or else standing waiting for the bus. It made her chilblains itch thinking of it; she always got them so bad in the winter. And then the lift would come up, and she'd have to start serving. And what with the noise, by the time the boy came to take over she'd be tired right out.

"Why, whatever's the matter with my Jeannie?" That would be Mum, seeing her sit so dumb at the table of an evening.

"It's awful, Mum. It's the noise, it's awful. And the way all them come through at the rush-hours, all so tired and so sad-looking, it makes you feel awful, reely it does. You can't 'elp feeling sorry for them, reely you can't, and it takes it right out of you."

Mum gave her a queer look then, and told her to pop off up to bed.

"It's the standing about," Dad said. "Gets 'er run down."

"It's as if there's such a lot of sadness in the world, and such a lot of sad people.... Oh, I don't know."

Once she said something like that to Norah. "It's as if you'd just got to stand there and get it all thrown at you, what they're all feeling like."

But Norah only said she was dotty.

It was awful those cold evenings. Sometimes when it was a fog, and as if it was night all day long almost, with the lights on. She used to start earlier than ever waiting for them to come, waiting for when she'd begin to feel them coming. She'd stand there rubbing her chilblains, rubbing one leg with the other foot. Then the lift crashed open and made her jump. That's them already. So it wasn't so bad to-day.

But it was only one fellow. "Box of vestas." She could have screamed.

He threw down the coppers, and then he drew off a step and lit his fag. A big, swanky fellow with a flash pin in his tie. And then swaggered off out to the street. And all he was thinking about was what he'd lost at the dogs, but he didn't mean anyone to know it.

There. Now. No it wasn't, not yet.

She really could have screamed.

All at once the lift crashed open, full up. It wasn't so bad then, once they'd got there: they'd soon be gone through. It was the waiting for them—that was what she minded. She was kept busy now serving one and another; it kept her mind off it, off the noise, and all them pushing past. Once she saw that one—the shy one—but he didn't speak; he was too shy. And then later on it got a bit quieter again, only the noise of the lift went on, going up and down. Every time the doors crashed it made her scream almost.

She'd be dropping nearly by the time she got home. And one time she put her head down on the kitchen-table and cried, just when Mum was putting on the tea.

"It's all that standing about," Dad said. "It's too much for 'er."

Mum got worrying over Jean then. She didn't know what to do. There weren't so many jobs going you could throw up a good one when you got it.

"Don't you go fretting, Mum. It's only the noise tires you out. I'll get used to it, I expect."

Mum shook her head, but she didn't see what she could do.

Jean used to try not to think about it. She used to try to tell herself stories to cheer herself up, so she wouldn't notice the noise when it came all of a sudden, and all the sad-looking ones there were. Those two over there, she'd say, he's taking her ticket for her, they're going up to the pictures, he's ever so fond of her, and they'll get married one day soon.

But then she'd go thinking—she couldn't help it, it was as if something said it to her—and then she'll let herself go, and get like that one coming in with the shopping-bag, and then he'll get tired of her and get someone else, and she'll get nagging at him when he comes home.

It wasn't any use.

And she couldn't stop herself waiting for the noise the lift-doors made, crashing back. As soon as the bell went down below, which meant a train was come in, and the lift started whirring, coming up, she'd hold on to the counter to stop herself from screaming, waiting for it. And then when it did come she'd go hot and cold all over, and her knees sharking so she could hardly stand up.

Then there was one day her chilblains were hurting her something cruel, and she'd got a cold in her head, and it seemed as if the lift was up and down, and someone wanting something, every two minutes.

She could have screamed, long before middle-day, and after the lunch-hour it dragged on and on, as if the day was never going to end. It was raining worse than ever; it was one of those days when everyone who came in seemed to bring a smell of wet with them.

Getting on for five o'clock it started to fill up, full of dripping umbrellas and macks, and some that hadn't got their macks with their clothes soaked through, pretty well. When the lift scraped up so slow, heavy and noisy, she could have screamed right out.

"Large Gold Flake," "Ten Players," "Box matches, miss." She stood slapping them out, waiting for the next lot to come up. There wasn't anyone at the counter for a minute, and she stood listening through the noise for the bell to go down below, and when it did she went hot and cold all over and the lights went out.

And then Mum was saying, "I'm much obliged to you, sir, I'm sure"; and someone was putting his hat on, going out of the door. And Mum was back, giving her something in a cup. "There, drink that up, Jean lovey."

"It's the standing about," Dad said. He was sat down having his tea at the kitchen-table.

The chair was hurting her leg; she was sat along on two chairs, over by the dresser. "Whatever 'appened?"

"Never you mind, lovey. You was took bad, and a gentleman brought you 'ome in 'is car."

She shut her eyes again.

"Why don't you get 'er into bed?" Dad said.

Mum kept her home next day, and took her to the doctor soon as the surgery opened, nine o'clock. Norah had to take Doris to school, and she didn't half grumble. "She oughter go by 'erself, a big girl like her."

The doctor said it was anæmia, and her nerves were bad, and she ought to give up working till she was better.

"It's only the noise, I'll get used to it presently, I expect." She felt so weak she didn't know what she was doing.

He said she ought to give up that work and get a quiet sort of job. So Mum wouldn't let her go back anymore; she kept her at home helping about the house, when she wasn't lying down upstairs. She used to lie there, and just stare at the wall and the way the window-blind was pulled up crooked. Sometimes she used to wish she could see things, to pass the time, like when she was little.

Sunday week Auntie Lil came, and she was surprised when she saw Jean, the way she'd got thinner than ever, and so white. And Mum told her all about Jean fainting and being brought home from work, and what the doctor said.

"So what you going to do with 'er now?"

"Keep 'er home a bit; it's the only thing."

Jean helped Mum clear away the dinner and make a cup of tea, and then she came back and sat with her and Auntie Lil. Dad had gone out for his stroll and Norah was upstairs dressing and Doris had run out to play.

Auntie Lil had got ever so stout, but she always looked nice, and always had a smile for anyone. It did you good to look at her.

She sat there stirring the sugar into her tea and giving Jean a look over across the table. "What you ought to do," she told Mum—"you ought to put 'er with Madam Eva."

"Where's that?" said Mum. "In the millinery?"

Auntie Lil settled herself back in her chair; she was always fond of her comfort. "Mrs. Harsett. 'Madam Eva,' she calls 'erself in the trade—profession, I should say. That's only the name she goes by, if you understand me. But Mrs. Harsett—that's who she is—she's a great pal of mine, she and me often pops in one another's place to 'ave a chat. Now she's in the fortune-telling business— clairvoyante, I ought to say—Mrs. Harsett is: that's Madam Eva. They all 'ave to call themselves Madam something—"

Mum said quickly, "I wouldn't 'ave any of that."

"And I 'appen to know," said Auntie Lil, "that she's looking for a nice, quiet, refined sort of girl to 'elp her in the house and learn the business."

"You know my views," Mum said, pursing up her mouth.

"Come now, Janet," says Auntie Lil; "you aren't going to stand in the girl's way."

Mum wouldn't hear of it at first, but Auntie Lil talked her round.

And then Dad came in from his walk, and had to be told. "How d'you know the girl can do it? When she's got 'er there?"

"Never you worry over that. Mrs. Harsett—Madam Eva, that is—'ll soon find *that* out for 'erself. She'll let you know soon enough if Jeannie isn't any good to 'er. She's ever so spiritual"—and Auntie Lil gave Mum a look—"she'll talk for hours on end about the spirits. It'll give you the creeps sometimes the way she'll say all of a sudden, 'I can see someone lookin' over your shoulder,' she'll say. 'It's a good spirit watchin' over you.' She'll give me the creeps very often."

"Well," said Mum, "what about you, Jeannie girl? D'you want to go to 'er?"

Jean turned pink with them all looking at her all of a sudden. She sat twisting her fingers together under the table. If she went to this Madam Eva she might learn to see things like when she was little—see them when she wanted to. "I don't mind if I do."

B

The concrete floor of the fun-fair slopes down from the street between walls of distorting mirrors; the air grows hotter and closer, traffic noises are blurred, and the blare of a loud-speaker playing a dance-tune jumps up from the depths of the hall. A few youths are shuffling aimlessly around the slot-machines. In the farthest stuffiest corner is a walled-off cubicle: Astria, Palmistry. Inside the cubicle three women and a man are waiting in furtive apathy on a bench. A murmur of voices comes from behind a curtain. The loud-speaker and shuffling footsteps can be heard through the thin wall.

Behind the curtain Astria is sitting at a small, wobbly table. Her client's hands are laid on it palms up, fingers twitching with anxiety and the effort of keeping still.

Astria prods at the palms with a pencil. She is speaking in a quick, low-voiced monotone: "You are affectionate, home-loving, and of a refined disposition. You have artistic tastes and should do well employed at artificial flower making or in the millinery or any like calling."

At her elbow lies a shabby handbag beside a cup of slopped tea with a sodden biscuit in the saucer.

"You will make marriage between the ages of twenty-five and thirty...."

"Oo, but...."

"Now isn't there some man in your life isn't so well-off as 'e would like to be?"

"Oo, I don't know?"

"Well, this has so far prevented 'im from declaring 'is love, which he will do before long. You 'ave a long life and good health, and should live to a good old age."

The monotone stops abruptly. Astria raps down the pencil, sighs impatiently, and jerks her chair.

"What you said about that man—what's he look like?"

Astria jerks restively. "If you haven't met 'im already you're going to. I see marriage and a long life."

She gets up. "That'll be one-and-six."

The client starts, fumbles in her bag, slowly puts down the coins. "But that what you said—I didn't quite get it...."

Astria snaps, "Long life and happiness, that's all. Isn't that enough for you?"

"Oo. Oo, all right." She lingers a minute, then unwillingly blunders out.

The woman at the end of the bench gets up, hesitates, steps sheepishly to the still swaying curtain.

Suddenly Astria pushes out past them, with a look of cross dislike. She slams out of the cubicle, through the stuffy, shambling youths; makes a bolt for "LADIES."

III

Jean did love it, being at Madam Eva's. Madam Eva—she was Mrs. Harsett really; there was only Mr. and Mrs. Harsett there, the daughter Elsie being married and gone away—had a little basement flat in a nice quiet square, up in Bayswater. It was all painted up with blue paint outside, and in the front room, where Madam Eva used to consult, there was always a blue bowl with yellow flowers in the window. When you came along up in the street and looked down over it did look nice

Madam Eva was ever so nice. She was a bit like Auntie Lil to look at, only older; stoutish and kind-looking, with a lot of wrinkles in her face where she was always ready for a laugh; only she was short—a little bit of a thing—and she had her hair which was going grey, done up to head with a net all over. You'd have a feeling she could see right through you sometimes, the way she'd look at you. Sometimes when Jean put her breakfast down in front of her she'd give a look right past, and tell her, "You're in luck to-day, you are. There's a good spirit got up along with you." And then she'd give one of her chuckles over her cup.

Mr. Harsett was ever so different. He never had a smile for anyone. He had a long, thin face, and didn't say very much; he worked as a timekeeper with a firm up by Paddington. In the evenings he'd sit there and he wouldn't say anything hardly, though he was all right when he did speak to you. Jean liked him all right. He used to ask her to fetch his baccy for him from the little shop down on the corner. It made her think of the time when she used to work in the kiosk out at High Lanes—and my, wasn't she glad she'd done with that! When she got back in the kitchen with Madam Eva and Mr. Harsett—where they used to sit in the evenings; the front room being kept for clients—it was like coming home.

What she had to do mostly to start with was help in the house and run errands and answer the 'phone when clients rang up for appointments and tidy the front room. She loved doing that. There was the curtain hung over the door, that was all of gipsy embroidery with bits of looking-glass in it, and Jean used to rub up the little bits of glass with her duster because she liked to see them shiny. And there was the little low chair Madam Eva used for sittings, that had to be turned back to the window, and the arm-chair for the client, turned facing. "Always watch their faces," Madam Eva used to say. "You can tell a lot from faces if you look." She was going to start teaching Jean later on. And there was the little table in the corner that had the crystal on, stood all by itself on a black wooden stand. And Jean had to dust that too. She didn't dare to at first. She used just to stand and look, for fear of knocking it off. Oo, it was lovely, reely it was! It was all full of the loveliest colours, but Jean couldn't see anything else in it, not yet, except for her own face looking down. Then she had to start some time, so she started one day dusting over the top of it ever so careful. But it seemed firmer on the stand than you'd have thought, so she gave it a good dust up till shone beautiful. Being here in Madam

Eva's room with the crystal looking so lovely, and being able to pick it up, even, when she wanted and look in it it—and Madam Eva was going to show her how to and with the packs of cards stacked neatly away in the drawer underneath, and all looking so bright in spite of the grey walls outside, with the yellow flowers—marigolds they were—looking like sunshine in the window, and Madam Eva so kind and nice—Jean felt as if she'd found herself.

One morning when she hadn't been there very long she was getting the front room tidy because there was a client coming, rang up at breakfast-time. The room was left since Madam Eva'd seen someone in it the day before, with the little table dragged out in front of her chair, and the cards spread out on it. Jean pushed the door to and draped up the curtain first, looping it up higher over the cord so that it hung nice. She ran her finger round one of the little bits of glass that were let into the embroidery—she did love this gipsy curtain—and then gave the glassy bits a good rub up with the duster. After that she went over and dusted the window-sill and picked off one of the marigolds which was dead, and crushed it up to throw away when she went out into the kitchen.

When she got round to the little table where the card were spread about all untidy she packed them up neatly and slipped the pack in the drawer; and then she was lifting up the table, with the crystal on it, to stand it back against the wall, when all at once she put it down again and picked the crystal up instead.

She hadn't ever had it right up in her hand like this before, only rubbed it over, like, while it was on the stand. It did look lovely too. The crushed-up flower she'd still got hold of was making a mark on it; she dropped the green and yellow bits on the table and rubbed the crystal over with her sleeve, and then she lifted it right up and looked into it. She did wish she could see something. Madam Evan was going to start teaching her any day now. She could see herself in it, and bits of the room, but that was only reflections.

She rested it on the back of the arm-chair and bent over and looked as hard as ever she could—and all at once it was as if it went dark, and she could see herself, dressed lovely, standing up in a big room with a light on her, and people sitting all round as if she was talking to them.

Then there was a noise, and she jumped and opened her eyes; and she wasn't looking in the crystal at all, but right at her own face in the glass over the fireplace, and she was ever so white, as if she'd seen a ghost. She just stood and stared at herself, kind of dazed.

It was Madam Eva had come in. She was standing up behind Jean's shoulder and chuckling at her, at the way she was looking. "You've got it all right"—giving her a pinch on her bottom—"you've got it!"

Jean did love Madam Eva.

She was always teasing Madam Eva to let her learn the crystal. "You don't want any teaching," Madam Eva told her. "You've got it all right!"

But Jean kept on teasing; she did so want to start. So one afternoon when there wasn't anyone, Madam Eva brought it out for her and put it on the kitchen-table.

It gave Jean quite a start when she turned round from the sink and saw it there, all alone on its stand on the table where she'd just cleared away the dinner things, with the dresser behind with the dishes piled up. "Oo, Madam Eva, you oughtn't to 'ave brought it out 'ere, did you?"

Madam Eva did laugh at her; her face went all puckered up. The way she had of laughing, without making any noise to speak of. "You get on. If you can't see things in a kitchen you can't see 'em in a droring-room. Get along with you!"

Only that wasn't what Jean meant, quite. It was as if it was something holy. Like taking something out of a church and putting it on the kitchen-table.

Madam Eva made her sit down then and put her elbows on the table, with the crystal in between them. And then she went and made herself comfortable in her basket-chair by the fender.

"Now if I didn't know you'd got it in you, mind, I never would be telling you all this. And mind, there's plenty would pay high to hear what I'm telling you. But I know you got it in you, girlie, I've seen it many a time. You're going to go far, if you listen to what I tell you."

"Yes, Madam Eva?"

Jean was staring down hard at the crystal; she couldn't help squinting. She could see herself small and bent crooked in the top of it, where there were the blue lights; and round the sides, where it was greyish and yellow, you could see the grain of the wood the kitchen-table was made of.

"Now when you got your client there you give it to 'er—it's mostly a 'her'—to hold. She's sitting down opposite you. You ought to be sat the other way about, back to the window, then you can see 'er face better. There's a lot can be learnt from faces. Now when you got 'er—don't look too much as if you're looking, mind—and sum 'er up in your own mind. How old is she, and what money's she got? You'll have to sum that up quick when you got clients regular. Remember this, though—everyone wants money, it doesn't matter how much they got. That's always a safe one. Now you take a good look at 'er, it'll give you a line to go on. Has she got a wedding ring on? You'll notice that first go off. But some take it off, she might have a mark there. You'll get to know all that by practice—nothing like practice. You can't do it all at once."

Jean looked up from the crystal. She hadn't seen anything yet, she was waiting for Madam Eva to tell her how. She'd looked at it so hard she couldn't stop squinting, she had to look across out of the window where there was the back-yard and the door of the coal-house.

Madam Eva shifted herself in her chair. "Now as for how long you leave it with 'er, that depends on the customer. You'll have to be watching 'er, and don't look as if you were, mind. Some that's the nervous sort will be ready to listen in a minute, soon as you've got them summed up. If it's the kind that doesn't believe in it and wants to catch you out the only thing is leave them longer. Most will get a creepy feeling if they're left 'olding the crystal long enough, and even if they don't they'll feel silly and want to put it down. Then they'll be glad to sit quiet and hear what you got to say.

"Now when you think it's time—and nothing but experience will tell you that—you take it from them and put it on your lap, or on the table—on a cushion, many do, it stops the reflections—and then you look into it."

Jean was staring hard out of the window; she could hardly breathe with waiting. "Yes, Madam Eva?" She gave a sigh. It was as if she was drifting away on something.

"Well, then you look hard at it, and by now you've got your client summed up all right, or you ought to have, and if you're lucky the idea comes to you which puts you on the right track. Then once you've started you can go on."

Madam Eva fidgeted in her chair and settled herself again. "That's what nobody's going to teach you, and what nobody can *teach* you, I don't care who it is, how the idea comes to you or where it comes from. The spirits bring it to you or else they don't. And if they don't God 'elp you! Mostly it just flashes into your mind: 'This woman's worrying over her husband's job,' or else, 'This one's lost her man; she wants to know if she'll get 'im back,' or one thing or another. Nobody's going to tell you where that comes from; *I* can't tell you. That's the clairvoyance—that's where it comes in; that's what you've got or else you 'aven't. All I can tell you, and all anyone can tell you, is how to make do when you've got a client sat there and it doesn't come."

Then she looked up at Jean, and then she turned round sharp and stared at her.

Jean opened her eyes and sighed, and when she saw the

back-yard she turned her head round slowly, and there was Madam Eva looking at her. "Oo, Madam Eva, I know I can do it. Something just told me I can."

Eva gave her a sharp look, and then she chuckled.

Jean jerked herself up out of her drowse; she never ought to get sleepy with Madam Eva going to tell her. She sat up straight and put her elbows back on the table. "Now tell me 'ow I ought to look in it; I'm looking now, look."

Madam Eva gave one of her laughs, and got up slow. "Go on, no one ever saw anything in the crystal, and don't you believe it. It's only to 'elp you to concentrate, that's all it is—aid to concentration. You got to see it in your own mind."

Jean looked up then, and Madam Eva was coming to the table, taking the crystal away in her little fat hands that had the rings on. One of them was a lucky ring, too, it helped you to be psychic. Jean was all in a daze still. "But Madam Eva, can't I go on trying?"

Eva gave her a push with her elbow and chuckled at her. "Get along, don't you go fretting over it. You've got it all right. You've got a lot some would give their eyes for—some that I could name. You don't want any teaching, you've got it there now, got it right inside your 'ead."

Jean was all in a daze. She watched Madam Eva hold up the crystal and give it a rub with her sleeve. She was going on talking to herself, something like, "And God 'elp you if you ever lose it." And then she made Jean go and have a lay-down.

When she woke up it was getting dark; she could only just see the coal-house door standing ajar in the yard outside the window. The water was running in the kitchen-sink the other side of the wall. It was Mr. Harsett washing himself; you could tell by his boots stamping on the floor when he moved round looking for the towel, and you could hear the regular swish of the water flatten out and splash when he put his head under the tap. Come in for his tea. She ought to go and help Madam Eva. She was ever so depressed because she hadn't seen anything in the crystal when Madam Eva was telling her. Fancy if Madam Eva was to say she wasn't any use and send her home. Oo she never would, would she?

She went in and helped to give Mr. Harsett his tea. She didn't say any more about it to Madam Eva, because Mr. Harsett didn't like a lot of business-talk when he was at home. He sat down and had his tea at the kitchen-table, and then a lady came unexpected for Madam Eva, and after Jean had answered the door and shown her into the front room she went back and washed up, while Mr. Harsett read his paper.

Later on when the client had gone Mr. Harsett went out to see his friend he talked to about horseracing, and then Jean was going to say something, only she didn't like to. And then Auntie Lil dropped in to have a chat with Madam Eva.

"You're quite a stranger," Madam Eva told her, and sent Jean to put the kettle on to make her a cup of tea.

"How's Jeannie getting on?" was the first thing Auntie Lil wanted to know. "The child looks as white as a ghost."

Jean was ever so depressed; she could have started to cry. She was going to tell Auntie Lil all about it, bow she couldn't do it, when Madam Eva chipped in first. "Doing fine. We'll make something of 'er yet!" Giving Auntie Lil a wink.

Jean was ready to cry. "I 'aven't seen a thing in the crystal yet."

Auntie Lil looked ever so surprised and sorry, and as if she didn't know which to believe.

But then Madam Eva gave one of her chuckles, and leaned over and smacked Jean on the back so that it made her choke almost. "She's got it all right, she's got it! She doesn't know 'er luck!"

The 'phone bell went then, out in the passage, and Jean had to go and answer. She heard Auntie Lil say, "Is she suiting you all right, then?" But she didn't hear what Madam Eva answered.

It was a lady wanting an appointment at twelve o'clock to-morrow.

When she got back in the kitchen Auntie Lil and Madam Eva were talking about something else. Then Mr. Harsett came in soon after, and Auntie Lil started chaffing him. Him and Auntie Lil were quite pally, though you would never have thought it, would you? "Tell us what's going to win next Saturday then."

He'd pretend not to know, and then Auntie Lil would wheedle it out of him, sitting there with the bunch of parma violets jumping up and down on the thrown-back collar of her coat with the way she talked and laughed. "All right then, you put a tanner for me on Whistling Top!"

When she went she told Jean, "Bye-bye, you be good!"

When Jean got to bed she tried to think what Madam Eva told her about how you ought to look in the crystal, but she couldn't remember one thing; and then she dropped off.

Next day, after she'd let the lady in at twelve o clock, she listened for a minute at the door to try and hear what Madam Eva was saying to her, but it didn't tell her anything. It was only after dinner, when Mr. Harsett had gone out again to work and Jean had cleared away and made the tea and Madam Eva was settled down with her cup in the basket-chair, that she started telling Jean again. "You go and get the cards. The pack out of the drawer."

Jean got up without a word. She could have cried. So that meant Madam Eva wasn't going to show her the crystal anymore. She went in the front room, where the table was pulled out by Madam Eva's chair and the cards thrown about all over it. She picked them up and tidied them and put them in the drawer, and then she took out the other pack that Madam Eva told her, and came and put them on the kitchen-table and sat down without a word.

"What's the matter?" Madam Eva asked her. "Don't you want to learn the cards?"

It was as much as she could do to keep the tears back. Madam Eva was looking at her hard, and she had to say something: "Aren't you going to show me the crystal anymore? I will try, reely I will."

Madam Eva gave a chuckle then, and told her all about it—what she ought to have heard the day before if she hadn't come over funny: how you didn't see in the crystal, but in your head, the way Jean did. "And that's a thing no one can't teach you, but you've got it all right. The good spirits gave it to *you*!"

Jean couldn't believe her ears at first, what Madam Eva was saying. How she was what they called a natural clairvoyante, that saw things all by themselves in their head without any teaching, and how she only had to learn now to concentrate and take notice, to be able to see it about the person who was inquiring.

"What you've got to learn now is the cards. Most wants that, or else the palmistry, or both; it comes cheaper for them than the crystal."

Madam Eva got up from her chair and put down her cup on the dresser and came over and sat down opposite Jean. She took up the cards and cut the pack—"Always cut with your left 'and, nearest the 'eart"—and showed her how to lay them out. "That's for the client, for 'er 'ome, for what she don't expect; and that one's the surprise. Always pay attention to that one, particular, you should."

She scrabbled up the pack and passed it over to Jean and told her to shuffle.

"Ar," she said, "you 'aven't got the feel of it yet."

Jean was awkward with the cards; she couldn't do it quick and neat like Madam Eva. She dropped one, and Madam Eva picked it up and nodded her head over it quite a bit, and then she made Jean slip it back among the others and shuffle again and cut and give her the pack.

"For you, for the 'ouse, for what you don't expect..."

Madam Eva sat and nodded over the cards as they came up; sometimes she pursed up her mouth and looked at one extra hard, and then she'd put down the next and go on, nodding again. Jean could see over her head into the yard outside, where there was a cat standing up on its hind-legs, trying to look in the dustbin.

When Madam Eva had done setting out the cards she looked up and gave Jean a hard stare. "There's a lot more than you think for, comin' to you—and a lot of good luck."

Jean jumped at that. "Oo, Madam Eva, is it for me, then? Tell me all there is there, do."

Madam Eva gave one of her chuckles down in her throat. "I'm not goin' to tell you all, or you'll be gettin' conceited. A lot of luck, and a bit of trouble too, like there is for most. But that won't"—-she pushed the cards about—"that won't amount to much. That's to say, nothin' to speak of. Good luck, that's what I see most of for you."

Jean had got her eyes wide open now. "Oo, Madam Eva, does it say if I'll be getting married?"

Madam Eva gave another chuckle at that. "You'll get married all right, don't you worry. All in good time. Plenty of time to think about that."

Jean went pink. "Oo, Madam Eva, I only meant would I some time."

Madam Eva swept the cards together and knocked them into a pack—not the clumsy way Jean had to, pushing each one into place and dropping some before she'd done—and passed them over. "Now what we've got to do is see you know your job."

She made Jean lay out the cards then, and started telling her what each one was, and how you ought to string them together to make a reading. Jean tried hard to remember all the meanings, but she was sure she never could; Madam Eva told her she ought to write them out and learn them. They went on shuffling and laying out the cards until it began to get dark and Mr. Harsett would be coming in for his tea, and Madam Eva said there were a lot of ways you could lay the cards out besides that, and she'd show her some more another day.

When Jean got to bed that night she took out the bit of paper where she'd written down the meanings Madam Eva told her—a long journey, fortunate events, the rival—and said them over and over to herself for a bit before she put the light out.

After that Madam Eva made her practise every afternoon almost. Sometimes a client would come, and then when Jean had answered the door and shown the client into the front room and watched Madam Eva pat her hair, that was always tidy anyhow under the net, and set off along the passage with her little, short steps that made hardly any noise, she sat down again at the kitchen-table and started laying out the cards by herself the different ways she'd been shown, and saying over the meanings. Sometimes she wondered if they meant anything about *her* when she laid them out like that. But you mustn't tell it for yourself; it was unlucky, so they said.

And when she got a bit quicker with the cards and only needed to practise to get used to it Madam Eva started her off reading hands. She used to sit there and spread hers out in front of her and try to remember what she'd been told—head and heart and life, and it depended where they started from— and try to see the difference between her right and left. The left was what you were born with and the right was what you made yourself. And if you watched, the right kept changing, only it took years to show sometimes. Jean had a bit of the psychic star in her left hand, and she meant to grow it quite perfect in the right. She was working ever so hard.

Sometimes one of Madam Eva's friends that she knew professionally would drop in of an evening, and then Jean would keep quiet and listen to them talking and try to learn something. Often when they'd settled themselves with a cup of tea or a glass of port-wine they'd start exchanging notes about clients they had, and how things were going, how business was looking up with the slump. "Half as many again in a trade depression, always. Not what you'd think, is it? But it's always like that."

"Though I haven't had a lot of that sort myself. More young girls lately."

That was Madam Madge. Jean didn't like her very much. She was a thin, cross little thing, quite old, and always grumbling. If it wasn't her clients it was her husband, or her son that wouldn't do what she wanted him to. But mostly it was clients.

"And I'll tell you a funny thing," she said once—"I don't know if you find it the same: whatever sort I start with of a morning the same sort goes on coming all day long. Either it'll be all young girls, or else wives with a grouse, or four men in a string, wanting to know about betting or the stock exchange, until I could scream. I know the minute the bell rings it'll be another one of the same sort."

Jean used to think of that sometimes when she was going to answer the door. She'd stand still a minute before she opened, trying to feel who it was outside, whether it was a man or a woman and old or young, but she hardly ever got it right. Madam Madge must be no end psychic. Jean tried ever so hard, and she did get it right once or twice.

Then there was Mr. Mitch the astrologer; he had a place up in the City—Professor Norman Mitch. He used to come in now and then of an evening and have a drink with Mr. Harsett and Madam Eva; and then presently Mr. Harsett would say he had to go out, and Madam Eva would give Mr. Mitch another glass of wine, and they'd talk over any clients she'd had lately that wanted astrology. Madam Eva didn't do astrology very much—you couldn't do everything—but now and then a client would want a horoscope cast, and then she'd get in Mr. Mitch to help her.

One night he was there, and Mr. Harsett was out, and Jean was watching him and Madam Eva while she washed up the supper things. They were sitting over the table, casting a horoscope. Mr. Mitch was a bit fat, with a white face, and his hair was curly except that he oiled it down, and starting to go bald on top, he brushed it across. He had a big ring on his little finger that flashed up when he kept flicking over the pages of the book—the "Ephemeris," they called it—that they were working out of. Madam Eva would go round when he was coming, slapping over the old books and papers that were on the dresser and thrown down on the floor by her chair—"Where's that blasted 'Phemeris go to?"—and Jean would have to find it for her.

Mr. Mitch smiled a lot, and he always called Madam Eva "My dear lady" when they were arguing. And he talked beautiful.

She'd say, "Give it 'ere; you 'aven't got that right," and snatch the book from him, all quite pleasant, and start turning it over. And then in a minute she'd say, Drat the thing!" and throw it down again on the table. Then Mr. Mitch would reach across for it, giving a laugh at her, quite quiet—"Pardon me, my dear lady"—and open it out again and show her the place.

Jean didn't really like Mr. Mitch very much; he had a funny way of looking at you.

When they'd done casting the horoscope Madam Eva got up and threw the books back on the dresser out of the way, and then she caught sight of Jean watching from where she was wiping her hands, over by the sink. "Come on over 'ere. Show Mr. Mitch 'ere 'ow you're gettin' on."

Mr. Mitch turned round and gave Jean a look; it made her go all hot in the fact the way it always did when he looked at her. When Madam Eva told her to come on and not be all day about it she put down the towel and came forward a step, and then she stopped again.

"Come on," Madam Eva called out. "Come and show what you been doin'."

"What've you got her on now," Mr. Mitch asked, giving her a look up and down. "Palmistry? Ah. Well, suppose I have a look at *her* hand now."

"Come on," said Madam Eva, moving round the table. "D'you think he's goin' to eat you?"

Jean stood wiping her palm up and down on her overall; it still felt damp from washing. Mr. Mitch was turned round waiting for her, he gave her one of his smiles.

"Come on, what's the matter with you?"

Madam Eva moved over, chuckling, and got behind Jean and gave her a push to make her go over to where Mr. Mitch was sitting at the table. She could feel her face go hot at the very idea, but she couldn't help but go.

Mr. mitch made her sit down by him; it made her ever so shy. "But this is a very psychic hand!" he said, quite surprised sounding, and Madam Eva chuckled and nodded at Jean.

"She'll go far," he said. "This young lady will go very far one of these days, if I'm not much mistaken."

She felt so shy she could have died.

"My dear young lady," he said, "I see a very big future before you, very big. Very great powers—sacred powers, if I may say so—which you must learn to use for the good of all. The good of humanity."

Jean didn't know where to look. Just think of it, him saying that! Mr. Mitch too—just think of it! She got up feeling all of a tremble, and went over quickly to put the kettle on for the cup of tea Madam Eva always had about ten o'clock of an evening. She was glad to have something to do, so that she hadn't got to stay and listen to him. Well, I never.

"Well," she heard Madam Eva say, "what d'you think of 'er?"

She only heard Mr. Mitch begin, "If you want my opinion, my dear lady"; and then she was so confused at having Mr. Mitch and Madam Eva talking her over like that between them that she dropped the lid of the kettle and didn't hear any more. As soon as the kettle was on the fire she slipped out and went into her own little room next door and shut herself in.

She couldn't get to sleep for a long time that night for thinking of Mr. Mitch, and how he'd said she was very psychic and had sacred powers. That was like Mum used to say—that you ought to think of it being something sacred. And if Mr. Mitch said she had it it must be true, because he was ever so good, Madam Eva always said. She'd always ask him to help her over the astrology, much more than she would Madam Madge. Mr. Mitch wasn't so bad, when you got to know him better?

After that Jean used to work ever so hard, practicing with the cards and reading hands with Madam Eva in the kitchen of an afternoon, in between clients, out of a book Madam Eva had with pictures of the different types in it. "Don't you go thinkin' you'll ever see one of them on any 'uman, though. If you did there wouldn't be a thing to it—any fool could do a readin' right off. Mixed, that's what they are, everyone—the same as people. You might see a thousand 'ands, and everyone different. That's where experience comes in."

Madam Eva was going to let her take on a client someday soon, to start getting experience, because that was the only way you could learn, really. Jean was ever so frightened at the very idea of a client; sometimes when she let one in she used to think how awful if she had to go in and tell her fortune for her. You mustn't say "tell a fortune," though—that was low-down; "do a reading," you must say. Jean wouldn't like to do a reading for that one, with the beads hung all over her. She looked as if she'd turn nasty if you didn't get on quick enough. Jean did admire Madam Eva, the way she went trotting in with a smile whoever it was. Some of the men looked easier, shy-looking, and frightened, as if someone was going to see them coming in.

Once when Jean'd slipped on her beret and run out to fetch something along at the shops there was one hanging round up the top of the steps, as if he didn't know whether to go on down or not. When he saw Jean he turned round and walked off as if he'd only been passing by and stopped a minute. He put her in mind of that shy one that used to come to the Tube out at High Lanes. If he was there when she got back she'd ask him if he wanted to see Madam Eva, just to help him out.

She slipped on down to the shops, and when she got back he wasn't anywhere about. They did that very often; came two or three times before they'd make up their minds to go in. But when she looked down over she could see his head and Madam Eva's over the curtain in the front room; she was reading the cards for him. So he'd managed to take himself in, after all.

Often at night she'd put the light out and sit looking at the dark out of the window. When you looked hard you could see where the top of the wall was, across the yard, and there was a tin roof in the yard on the other side of the wall, you could just see it, and it used to catch the light if there was a window lit anywhere, especially if it had been raining. Jean used to sit and look at that bit of light reflected on the tin roof in the next yard, because you had to have something like that to help you to concentrate—that was what Madam Eva used to say, and that was what the crystal was for. If you looked hard at something long enough you'd go off, if you were lucky, and see things.

Jean would sit and look at the shiny bit of roof until it seemed like it came up close and got all big and misty; and she'd have seen something in a minute, only someone put the light out that was shining on the roof, and that brought her back. Once when she came back it was as if she'd been speaking, saying something, only she didn't know what. Like when you wake up sometimes after you've been dreaming. She'd have to ask Madam Eva what it meant when you did that.

She was going to ask Madam Eva at breakfast-time, only Madam Eva'd got a cold in the head, dreadful, and she was sitting there at the table wiping her nose, with her eyes running, saying, "Godsakes, let's 'ope none of them takes it in their 'eads to come to-day."

Mr. Harsett had gone out, and Jean had just done making Madam Eva a bit of toast, when the 'phone bell went; and they both knew what it meant. "Drat it! There, what did I tell you? And another time there mightn't be one for days together."

"I'll tell them you 'aven't got any time, shall I? Booked right up?"

"That'll do. Go on. It goes right through my 'ead."

Madam Eva was sitting there holding her ears, for the bell going on ringing. And then just when Jean was taking down the receiver she scraped her chair back and called out to her, "Book it."

"Oo, but Madam Eva——"

"Book it, I tell you. Book it." And then she blew her nose so loud Jean could hardly hear in the 'phone. It was a lady wanting twelve o'clock. Favourite time that; they slipped in just before they went back home to dinner.

When she got back Madam Eva was sitting there rubbing her eyes with her knuckles.

Jean brought her the toast. "But Madam Eva, you never can."

"Go on with you. *You'll* do it."

"Me! Oo Madam Eva, I never could! Reely I couldn't."

Jean could have died. She would have run away that minute, anything. "*Reely* I couldn't, Madam Eva, *reely*. Suppose she was wanting the crystal, or if I had to do the cards and didn't remember—no reely, Madam Eva, reely I couldn't!"

"Get along with you." Madam Eva reached out for the butter. "Got to start some time, 'aven't you? Well, then."

Jean didn't know what to do. Madam Eva wasn't like herself to-day; it was from having a cold. She was ever so cross.

She didn't know whatever she was going to do. She went and put the front room straight, and when she thought of sitting there in Madam Eva's chair it made her come out in a cold sweat.

She went and asked Madam Eva if she couldn't put the lady off when she came, but Madam Eva wouldn't let her; so she asked her what she ought to do to get ready.

"Get and tidy yourself up. And don't fidget yourself, you little fool!"

She went and tidied herself fifty times before twelve o'clock, and then the lady was late. When she did ring and ask for Madam Eva, Jean was in such a fright she just showed her in the same as usual and went back to the kitchen, where Madam Eva was leaning round in her chair to see who it was. "Oo, Madam Eva, reely I can't!"

"Get on, you little fool!"

But Madam Eva was giving a chuckle; she couldn't help it, the way Jean looked. She came round the table and gave her a push. "Go on, that one's easy, I can tell that. Give her cards; don't forget the wish. Got to start some time."

She came along the passage behind Jean and gave her a pinch to encourage her when she'd got hold of the door-knob. "Go on, you'll be all right."

Jean slipped in; she hardly knew how to stand up. When she had pulled the door to the curtain fell back across it, shutting her into the room.

The lady looked round. "Oh, it's you again," she said. "But you aren't Madam Eva, are you?" She was quite elderly, with a made-up face.

Jean didn't know what to do; Madam Eva never told her what to say. "Madam Eva's ill," she said; "I'm sorry." She could feel her mouth stiff when she talked. Then it was as if she could hear Madam Eva telling her. "I'm Madam Jean," she said. "Would you like me to do a reading for you?" She sat down in Madam Eva's chair, it felt safer with her arms on the table.

You could see the client didn't like it very well: "You're very young, aren't you?"

Jean didn't say anything. She pulled out the drawer and felt for the cards. If only she could get them laid out she might remember something. But when she'd got the packs on the table and looked up the lady was taking off her gloves. "I'll have palmistry, I think. Do you do the crystal?"

You could see she was used to it. Now if it had only been someone young...

"Crystal's very expensive," she said. She could feel the sweat breaking out. "It's a guinea, the crystal. You can 'ave the cards for five shillings, if you like—or palmistry. But if you 'ave that and the crystal too it'll be twenty-six shillings."

"All right, I'll have the two, then."

So that wasn't going to put her off.

The lady hitched her chair up. "Now then, mind you tell me all you see. I don't want anything kept back." She put out her hand for Jean to read it.

Well, she didn't have to do anything in the house, you could see that. Married to someone with enough money, then. Jean started off reading her lines for her, as well as she could remember, by the book, making it last out. She didn't know whatever she was going to do. But she couldn't put it off forever. In the end she had to give the client the crystal to hold.

She hardly knew how to take it from her and put it on the stand, she was shaking so. And when she looked there wasn't anything in it. She bent down over it and shut her eyes tight till her head was swimming and she hardly knew what she was saying, telling the lady about her rich husband and how he was going to get richer and the prosperous life she was going to have. "You've 'ad trouble," she said; "it hasn't always been so easy." You could see she wasn't any class.

She felt her head going hot with trying to concentrate, and when she couldn't do it anymore she looked up, the way Madam Eva had told her to, and said, "Is there any question you'd like to ask me?"

The lady was sitting holding on to her pearl necklace. "You aren't bad. But you haven't told me anything about my Benny."

She bent down over the crystal; she could feel herself sweating. Nothing more came to her. He must be her son, mustn't he? It wasn't even cloudy now, all got clear again and reflecting the room and her sitting there with her fat feet in her high-heeled shoes. Only suppose he wasn't, and she got it wrong…

And then all at once it was as if a drop like a tear fell on the crystal and rolled down over it. That must be one of the signs like Madam Eva said, if you were lucky! She started off ever so fast then: "I see sorrow coming for him and for you…" Running down over where she was sitting. "But it's going away; it'll all be clear in a minute. Won't take long before it all clears up."

She couldn't do anymore to save her life. "It'll all clear up," she said; "it won't take very long." She sat back. There wasn't anything else.

"Well," said the lady, getting up, "you've taken a weight off my mind."

When she'd gone Jean went straight out to the kitchen to Madam Eva and sat down in the chair, she was so fagged out. "I'll never do that again, never! It takes it right out of you; you can't hardly stand up!"

Madam Eva did laugh at her, and so did Mr. Harsett; he'd come in to dinner. "What d'you want to work so 'ard at it for?" Madam Eva asked her. "You gave 'er much too long. And just look at yourself!"

They made her look at herself in the glass, and she was as white as a sheet and the sweat standing out in drops all over her forehead and running down. Jean had to laugh too, but she did feel shaky,

And then when Mr. Mitch came in that night Madam Eva got chaffing, telling him about it, how Jean had got all in a sweat over seeing her first client. But he was ever so sympathetic, he didn't even laugh at her. He said it was always like that when you began; it took it out of you dreadful when the spirits got hold of you. Jean had quite got to like Mr. Mitch, even though he did look at you funny sometimes.

After that Madam Eva made her see a client now and then, some of the odd ones, when it wasn't regulars. Some of them didn't like it very well, her looking so young, and sometimes one would get quite nasty: "Now I'm not going to tell you anything. You needn't think I'll help you out."

"I don't want you to tell me anything, madam," she'd say, quite quiet. And sometimes they'd look ashamed of themselves.

Some would tell you everything straight away, without being asked. "Now I want to know about my daughter. She's keen on this married man— I won't tell you his name—but I do think it's a mistake myself. I often tell her, 'Irene, I do think these office romances are a terrible mistake, really I do; and suppose Mrs....' I mean, if his wife was to find out... I do think she ought to be careful, don't you? Because then she'd lose her job, and I don't know what we'd do at home."

Half the time they only wanted to be sympathized with; they didn't really want you to tell them anything. And that was where it would come difficult for her, because they'd say sometimes, sort of annoyed, "But you're too young to understand that."

That was what Madam Eva said too. They really wanted sympathy, and to be told all their troubles would come right. Madam Eva was ever so good at that herself; they'd all come and tell her their troubles and go away looking cheered up.

"Only what are you to do when the cards come out all wrong for them?"

Well, you just had to leave out the bad cards, then. But Jean didn't like the idea of that; it was like making the spirits tell lies. Sort of, wasn't it? It was different for Madam Eva; she had so much experience she could see far ahead and see how it would all turn out right in the end if you waited long enough. But Jean couldn't, very often, and she couldn't bring herself to make it up. "I do hope your troubles will all come right," she'd say, and the client would go off, grateful, but sad-looking. It wasn't often she could say, "You'll get all you want; it's all turning out right for you."

Madam Eva told her she wasn't much good at the cards because of it, and she ought to work up a line of her own—crystal, or trance, if she could do it. "You get a better class of clients on that. It might be more your style." Madam Eva was looking at her quite worried sometimes.

It made Jean feel worried too, to think she was letting down Madam Eva, after she'd been so good and done so much for her. She used to sit up worrying at night, and then she'd put the light out and sit in the dark practising her concentrating. Sometimes if she stared long enough at one point, a speck of light on the roof across the yard, or else the knob of the window-catch when it stood up black in the window after she'd looked long enough for it to get lighter outside, it would start coming up close at her, ever so close and misty, and she'd almost seem to go off in a dream. And sometimes there'd be pictures in it—the way it used to be when she was little; it might be a lot of trees or a lovely garden with flowers growing. Only when she came back she never could remember what she saw except for the first bit, and it did worry her. Often it was as if she'd been talking hard to herself all the time, and yet she couldn't catch what it was about. If only she could have made it out for once she might have seen where she was going wrong and what she could do about it. She never told that to Madam Eva, about hearing herself saying things, because she always hoped one day she'd be able to remember all about it and learn to read the crystal really properly, and then Madam Eva would be ever so pleased.

It was ever so much harder concentrating with a client there, when it was light and you felt them looking at you. She had to shut her eyes and hope it would go misty, and it did a bit sometimes, but she never could get right off the way she did when she was by herself. And she was half afraid to try it too, in case she couldn't remember enough to tell them when she came back. And most of them didn't want to wait either, they'd be popping questions at you all the time, "Tell me about my little girl—what she's going to do when she grows up"; or, "Aren't I going to get any luck coming to me soon?" Most of them wanted to know that.

It didn't happen until one day when a client came in—quite a girl, about Jean's age, she must have been, and so tired and worried-looking Jean couldn't help being sorry for her. She asked for the cards, but you could see it was only that she couldn't afford any more, for she kept looking at the crystal as if she'd give a lot to know what was in it and looking away again quickly.

"Would you like the crystal?" Jean asked her.

And she quite jumped. "Oh, no, thank you, the cards will do quite all right. I expect you can tell as much from them, can't you?" You could see she didn't believe it really.

Jean set out the cards and started off reading them to her, and then, while she was talking, all at once it was as if the cards went big and misty and faded out, and she was looking all along a road that had sunshine at the end of it. She didn't know any more until she came back the way she did when she was by herself and heard her own voice as if it had been talking. There were the cards still laid out in front of her, but she was sitting back in the chair and she hadn't moved them from the first layout, hadn't even turned up the wish.

She was going to do it when the girl got up and took her hand. "Oh, thank you," she said, with tears in her eyes. "You have helped me such a lot."

She put down her money and went out, and Jean went and told Madam Eva. She felt all in a daze.

"What did you tell 'er, then?"

"I don't know, reely I don't."

Well, Madam Eva couldn't believe it at first, and when she did she was so excited she had to ring up Mr. Mitch straight away and tell him how Jean'd gone off in a trance in a sitting, and how he must come round and hear about it.

Jean was standing in the kitchen all in a daze, and there was fat little Madam Eva out in the passage, at the 'phone, jumping up and down with her shoulders, the way she did when she was excited. "She's got it! Didn't I tell you she's got it!"

And when Mr. Mitch came round that night and heard all about it he said how Jean must be a natural direct-voice medium, and how Madam Eva never ought to have put her to anything else.

"I always told you she was," Madam Eva snapped out at him, "but she never did it before that I could prove."

Mr. Mitch didn't take any notice of Madam Eva snapping at him; he was looking at Jean as if he couldn't look hard enough at her. "My dear young lady," he said, "you've got a very precious gift. Very precious," he said.

It made Jean go hot the way he was looking at her and saying things like that, but he was ever so nice and kind.

C

"I see a lovely spirit lookin' over your shoulder, dear. A sweet young girl, and lovely blue eyes she s got and 'er 'air 'anging down 'er back. Such a lovely young gurl, and she's watchin' over ye-ew. She's tellin' you not to worry; it's all right. What?—don't you know 'oo she is? You think again. That's what she's sayin'. 'Don't yew worry; it's all right.' No? Well, p'raps you'll think of it presently.

"There's another one too—a man, that is, in a uniform. 'E says 'e was killed in the War. Well, you think; you'll know 'oo 'e is in a minute. An' there's an old lady too, dressed all in black with a big brooch on 'er front. Now, didn't your grandmother 'ave a big brooch like that, dear? Can't you remember 'er? What a shame! Well, that's 'oo it is; she's just said so, and she says to tell you she's watchin' over yew, an' everything'll be all right for you."

IV

Madam Eva was all for Jean going off in a trance then and there to show them, but Mr. Mitch wouldn't hear of it. He said they must fix it up and he'd come back another day when she was rested. And he wouldn't have Madam Madge asked either, or any of the others—not for the first time, in case it put her off, he said. He and Madam Eva ought to judge for themselves.

So he came back the next evening, and Mr. Harsett went out to see a friend, and Mr. Mitch and Madam Eva went and sat over in the basket-chairs the other side of the kitchen, and Jean was sat at the table. She was ever so nervous she wouldn't be able to do it.

Mr. Mitch was looking her over different from the way he always did, more in a sharp way. "Any signs of levitation?" he asked her.

Jean stared at him; she hadn't understood.

"Leave 'er alone," Madam Eva told him. "Let 'er do 'er stuff."

Jean sat there with the light glaring down on the deal table. She shut her eyes tight. It was awful with them looking at her; she couldn't forget they were there, even with her eyes shut. It was a long time before she could get off; she held her breath until it seemed as if she was going to faint. But then the next thing she knew she was coming round, and it was as if she could hear her own voice away off in the distance, but she couldn't move except to open her eyes. And there were the two of them, sitting forward staring at her. Madam Eva was sitting still as if she'd been shot, and so was Mr. Mitch, except that he was tapping his fingers on his knee.

And then Jean moved, and they looked round quick at one another.

"There, what about that! Has she got it, or 'asn't she?"

Mr. Mitch was looking at Jean soft-like now, not the hard way he'd been staring before. "She has indeed, my dear lady. Quite remarkable! She'll have to decide what she's going to do with it," he said.

Madam Eva gave him a sharp look then. "I'll ring round a few of my regulars and get up a little *séance* for 'er."

Mr. Mitch seemed to think, and then he turned round sharp on Madam Eva: "You can't do that. You want to get a more classy place. Start her off with a splash, up in the West End."

"And suppose it don't come off? What about the rent?"

"H'm," he said. He went on tapping on his knee.

"Eh?"

"Well," he said, "we'll have to see. All right, you try her out here."

"I'll try 'er out where I like, come to that."

Jean sat and looked from one to the other. She didn't know what they were arguing about. "Was it all right?" she asked, faint-feeling.

"What's that? First-rate. Now you run off and get a spot of shut-eye."

Mr. Mitch got up: "Just a minute, my dear young lady." He came over and stood quite close to her, playing with his watch-chain. "Just a minute before you go. Who's your guide?"

"Beg pardon?"

She looked round for Madam Eva to help her out.

"Guide?" said Madam Eva. "Ar, I forgot that."

"Your control," Mr. Mitch explained to Jean, giving her soft looks—"your spirit-guide. Who is it who speaks through you?"

"Oo, I don't know!"

Madam Eva got up then and came round the table to them. "Don't you go fussing 'er up. She doesn't need to know that."

Mr. Mitch turned round sharp on Madam Eva; you could see he didn't like her interfering. "My dear lady," he said, quite annoyed looking in a way, "if you're going to advertise a *séance*."

"Advertise nothing! I'm only getting in a few regulars."

Mr. Mitch looked as if he'd say some more, and then he turned round instead and patted Jean on the shoulder, encouraging. "There, there; this young lady will tell us another day. We mustn't ask too much, must we?"

Jean didn't like to go while Mr. Mitch was patting her shoulder, but as soon as he'd stopped and was stroking his watch-chain again she gave him a smile and went off to bed. She was dropping.

As she went out she heard Madam Eva say, "Well, I'll tell you what I'll do…" And then the kitchen-door shut.

Jean did like Mr. Mitch ever so, really.

She asked Madam Eva next day what it was Mr. Mitch meant, and what she'd done wrong. But Madam Eva said it wasn't anything she ought to have done; Mr. Mitch only wanted to know who was the spirit who was speaking, because when you went off like that in a trance and started talking it was a spirit that was talking through you and would bring along other spirits that wanted to talk to the sitters when you had sitters there. It must be some spirit that took a special interest in Jean and came along to help her.

Jean was quite bothered over it, not knowing. But the next time Mr. Mitch came along he told her just sit still before she went off and see if she couldn't see anyone.

So she shut her eyes tight and tried to make her mind a blank the way you ought to, only she couldn't; she couldn't help thinking, whoever would she see? And then after a minute or two, when it was starting to go misty, all at once she saw Doris in her mind, plain as plain. She could see her there, right in front of her, with the mist going round all round her. And she wasn't grown a big girl like she was the last time Jean went home, but the way she used to be—running along by the mailcart when she first learned to walk by herself.

So Jean opened her eyes and told Madam Eva, "I only saw our Doris."

Madam Eva quite jumped. "Why, she can't ever have passed over, bless 'er little heart!" She gave a look at Mr. Mitch.

Mr. Mitch wanted to know who it was. And when he heard he smiled quite kind at Jean. "You tell us what she's like," he said.

Jean told him how it was Doris when she was a little bit of a thing. "With 'er yellow curls, and 'er blue bow tying up 'er 'air. I saw 'er plain as plain."

"Splendid!" said Mr. Mitch. He didn't take any notice of Madam Eva. He put his head back and gave one of his laughs without making any noise, and then he sat up suddenly and slapped Madam Eva on the knee without even looking at her; he was looking all his eyes out at Jean. "Splendid, my dear young lady! Do you know who that was? That wasn't Doris; it was my little sister Daisy!"

A dreamy expression came over his face then. "I remember her as if it was yesterday."

Jean took it in at last—how it wasn't Doris she saw, but Mr. Mitch's little sister who passed over when she was a little bit of a thing; and Mitch was ever so pleased she'd come back to help Jean. And then he said, "Now, suppose you let us hear what Daisy's got to say to us."

Jean shut her eyes and thought hard about little Daisy Mitch till she could see her again clear, and went off almost at once; she was learning now how do it when she wanted, with holding her breath and thinking of clouds of smoke turning round, and when she came back Madam Eva was quite excited. "That's right," she told her, "that was Daisy all right. She said she'll be pleased to come and talk any time you like. She's a dear little thing."

Jean was ever so pleased about Daisy. It was like having a friend coming to help you. She'd try shutting her eyes tight and thinking hard about Daisy till she could see her quite clear, as if she is standing there in front of her. And very soon she only had to shut her eyes to see her straight off. Sometimes she used to think she'd hear Daisy say, "I want to talk now, Jee-een." And then Jean would look at her hard in her mind, until she came up big and close and faded out. And sometimes she'd kind of hear Daisy's voice going away in the distance as she came round.

Once it happened like that when Madam Eva was there, one time Jean was dusting round the front room. All at once she heard Daisy's voice say, away inside her head, "Jee-een, I want to now."

And it was as if everything was going black, she went and sat down in the nearest chair and let herself go off, and when she came round Madam Eva told her it was wonderful; you could hear it was Daisy talking—it wasn't like Jean's voice at all. She said Jean was ever so much better at it when Daisy came to help her. Only Jean mustn't do it too often, Madam Eva said, when wasn't anyone there, or she'd only wear herself out.

Madam Eva wanted to hold a *séance* for herself. Mr. Mitch was quite keen on it too now, only Jean was so frightened she wouldn't be able to do it with all those people round. Talking to a whole crowd like that!...

"But you must remember, my dear young lady," Mr. Mitch told her—it was one of the times he came to tea—"it isn't you who do the talking but our little friend Daisy. Don't you think she wants to talk to people? It isn't quite fair, is it, to hold her back?"

Madam Eva was pouring the water in the cup. "That's right,

that's what I say. You can't keep the poor little thing shut up like that, it's a shame."

"I'll tell you what," said Mr. Mitch, "we'll talk to Daisy herself, shall we? Let her say what she wants?"

"All right," Jean said. She had to say something, with them both going on at her.

So then Madam Eva passed over the brawn, and she and Mr. Mitch got on with their tea. Jean didn't, she only had a sip, she never could eat when she was anywhere near talking to Daisy. And not only that, she didn't know whether to laugh or cry, thinking she might have to get up at a *séance* and talk in front of a whole lot of people. She picked at the bits on her plate, hoping ever so that Daisy would say it didn't matter, that she'd as soon talk to Jean quiet, by herself.

Daisy didn't, though. As soon as they'd done and the table was cleared, Jean sat down and shut her eyes and went off. And when she came round she heard that Daisy had told Madam Eva and Mr. Mitch all about how she wanted to talk to a lot of people—the more the better, she said—to help them, because what she was there for was for helping people, and so Jean must let her talk to as many people as ever she could.

So after that Jean couldn't say any more against the *séance*, and Madam Eva rang round to some of her regular clients she had the addresses of and got them to come next Sunday.

Mr. Mitch got some of his clients to come, too. Jean stood in the kitchen Sunday afternoon and listened to the bell going and Madam Eva showing them into the front room. She was frightened out of her life of Madam Eva coming and fetching her. Mr. Harsett was sitting there in the kitchen having a pipe by himself and reading the paper; he didn't take any notice of her. The front room was full of people, and Mr. Mitch was in there. When the bell went and Madam Eva let another one in Jean could hear them talking as the door opened, and Mr. Mitch with his voice clear above all the others: "My dear lady..."

By the time Madam Eva did come to fetch her she was in such a fright she could hardly move. Madam Eva had to give her a push and a good hard pinch to get her along the passage, even. And then she reached around and opened the door, and Jean couldn't do anything else but go in. Everyone stopped talking.

Mr. Mitch showed her to a chair. The curtains were drawn, so that it was half dark, but you could still see the people sitting round. Some were whispering, but when Mr. Mitch stood up behind Jean's chair they stopped. Madam Eva had come in and was standing by the door.

Mr. Mitch started talking; he had a brown velvet coat on that Jean hadn't seen him in before. He was saying this was the new remarkable psychic they had heard about, and her spirit-guide, the little girl Daisy, was going to speak to them.

Jean was staring at their white faces all round in the half-dark; she was afraid to move. But when she heard Mr. Mitch say that, she remembered she had to go off, and she wondered whatever to do; she shut her eyes and thought harder about Daisy than she ever had in her life. It was awful. Daisy would seem to come and then she'd go off again. Somebody was whispering, "What a time she takes"; and Mr. Mitch whispered back, "Ssh, *if* you please."

Then she thought about Daisy again and made a tremendous effort to see smoke going round, and then she heard Daisy's voice far away, like at the end of a tunnel, and got off.

When she came back they were all talking again, in low voices. "I thought she was very good, didn't you?" "Most helpful." "You ought to have been with me last week, though..." But one was saying out loud, "I didn't understand a word of what she said about my husband's brother. Can't you tell her to say it again?"

Jean opened her eyes and saw Mr. Mitch move forward with his hand held up to stop her. "Pardon me, my dear lady, the medium has passed out of the trance state and cannot be questioned any further."

"I don't see why not. Why can't she go under again?" the lady went on complaining.

Mr. Mitch drew back the curtains, and Jean moved in her chair; she felt stiff the way she always did after she'd been off. Madam Eva signed to her that she could slip out, and as she went she heard them all start talking again at the tops of their voices.

She went out in a daze and sat at the empty kitchen-table. Mr. Harsett looked up. "Get on all right?" She didn't say anything, and he went on reading his paper. Jean put her head down on her arms. She heard the door open again, and their voices, and Madam Eva come out to fetch the tray of refreshments. Then she went to sleep.

When she woke up the first thing she saw was a glass of beer, and then she saw Mr. Mitch and Mr. Harsett and Madam Eva were sitting round the other end of the table having one apiece, and Mr. Mitch and Madam Eva were talking over the *séance*. They seemed quite pleased with the way it had gone off.

Jean sat up, and Madam Eva saw her and gave a chuckle. She was going to pass Jean a glass of beer, but Mr. Mitch stopped her. "My dear lady, alcoholic drink dulls the spiritual perceptions."

Mr. Harsett poured himself another glass and blew on it.

Jean asked, "What was that one saying, that she didn't understand? Didn't I do it right?"

Madam Eva said, "Don't you take any notice of her, the old bitch! She's one of that sort."

And Mr. Mitch said, "My dear young lady, there are always malcontents."

"Was it all right, then?"

"First-rate," Madam Eva told her. She fetched Jean a cup of tea from the stove and made her drink it. She gave a wink at Mr. Mitch. "We'll make something of 'er yet, won't we?"

It seemed as if Mr. Mitch and Madam Eva couldn't agree between them what she ought to do next. Mr. Mitch was coming round more and more often, and Jean would hear them sometimes, arguing over it. Madam Eva wanted her to take clients now and then for private settings and hold a little *séance* every other Sunday if they could get enough together. She said she'd put an advertisement in the local paper and the *Spirit Times*.

Mr. Mitch said she wasn't going to throw away what had fallen in her lap, and where Jean ought to be was up in the West End, with the sort of connexion he could get for her.

Madam Eva said, well, anyhow it was her lap it fell in and not Mr. Mitch's. And Mr. Mitch said he wasn't so sure about that. Madam Eva said, "Get on with you, you old goat!" and gave one of her chuckles, and then they started arguing again hard as ever.

Jean would hear them when she came back from answering the 'phone or fetching in the coal from the year. "Look here," Madam Eva would say, "you leave the girl alone."

Jean didn't see what Madam Eva wanted to be so nasty with him for when he was so nice and kind, and, after all, he was only saying what he thought.

And then it seemed as if they agreed between themselves, because Madam Eva stopped going on at him the way she used to and got all honey again.

She didn't say a word when Mr. Mitch asked Jean straight out one day if she wouldn't like to set up on her own and leave Madam Eva's. Jean only said, "Oo, I don't know!" She thought he was only fooling.

But then when he went on to say, quite serious, suppose Daisy wanted her to go where she'd be able to talk to a lot more people and have big *séances*, up in the West End, where Daisy could do twice the good, she got quite scared, and said she never could get on without Madam Eva telling her. Whatever would she do, all by herself like that?

Madam Eva shook with laughing when she said that, and Mr. Mitch went quite pink; he was always so pale. "My dear young lady," he began saying, but then he didn't go on anymore.

Jean wondered whatever she'd said.

When he was going she held his coat up for him to get into. And the way he took it from her he took her hand along with it, and held on so that she couldn't move it off.

She didn't like to pull away, in case he didn't know and it showed him what he'd done. So she stood there as if she was holding the coat up for him while he put the other arm in; she getting ever so hot, hoping she'd be able to move away quick when he'd done without him noticing; until he looked round over his shoulder and gave her a smile—he had lovely white, even teeth—and a look that meant he'd known all along.

She was so confused she felt the tears jump up in her eyes, and before she knew what she was doing she'd run right out of the kitchen and shut herself up in her own room. She could hear them both laughing at here.

She sat there with her heart beating fast from the way she'd run, and when it got slower she started wondering whatever made her do that, of all the silly things to do, because now she didn't like to go back in there, and she'd feel ever so silly having to see Mr. Mitch next time he came. And he'd be ever so hurt with her too.

Presently when he was going out past the door she heard Madam Eva say, "Well, you'll get that horoscope cast, then?" And Mr. Mitch said he would, right away.

So they hadn't gone on talking about here—that was one thing.

She was half afraid to go out to the kitchen again, for fear that what Madam Eva would say, but Madam Eva didn't take any notice of her. Only at breakfast next morning she told Jean, quite casual, that Mr. Mitch was going to cast a horoscope to find out what was best for Daisy. It made Jean feel worse than ever, to think she'd been so nasty to him.

He didn't show up for two or three days, and Jean did wonder, only she didn't like to ask. And then when he did turn up, it was an afternoon when Madam Eva had sent her out to shop, right over to Kensington High Street, to match up a bit of stuff or her, and by the time she got back he'd been there and gone. She didn't know whether to be glad or sorry.

"Disappointed, eh?" Madam Eva asked her.

And that made her go pink and look away; she didn't know how to take it.

"Don t you fret; he's coming back to-night. You see 'im all right then."

Jean took her things off and put them over a chair. "Did 'e say anything about the horoscope?" she asked, for something to say.

"He did." Madam Eva had one of her sly looks on. She went on with what she was doing, cooking Mr. Harsett's tea. "He'll tell you all about that to-night."

She kept her sly look on all through tea. But afterwards, when Mr. Harsett had gone out to see a friend, it seemed as if she thought better of it all of a sudden. She turned round straight and sharp on Jean, and told her, "Now don't you go playing up with your bashfulness when Norman Mitch is here to-night. You know what 'e's after all right, don't you?"   .

Jean didn't know where to look; she didn't know whatever Madam Eva could mean. To cover up her blushes she told her quickly, "I know all right. He's coming about the horoscope—to say what I ought to do about Daisy."

Madam Eva gave her a push. "Go on! You aren't such an innocent as all that. You know as well as I do he's crazy about you, and mind you don't play up silly; you mightn't get such a chance another time."

Jean felt as if she was going to faint. She couldn't believe her ears, what Madam Eva was saying to her. Mr. Mitch crazy about *her*! She couldn't have said a word to save her life. As if Mr. Mitch could ever want to look at someone like her!

"And you're fond of 'im, anyone can see that with 'alf an eye— yes, you are. It's only that you're young and don't know what you want. You could do a darn sight worse for yourself. He'll set you up in a way I couldn't—set you up with a West End clee-an-tale. Get you further than anyone else could that I know of. And don't you forget who it was got you your chance."

Madam Eva gave her a sharp look: "Well, what've you got to say?"

Jean couldn't have said a word if it was ever so.

Just then the bell rang, and before she knew it she'd run across and shut herself up in her own room. She knew it was Mr. Mitch, and she heard Madam Eva go to let him in, muttering to herself.

Jean stood behind the door in the dark, and heard them go by outside in the passage. She was shivering with the cold.

After a minute Madam Eva came across and told her to go in and speak to him. "Go on, you little fool. What're you scared of?"

She gave a chuckle then to cheer Jean up, and poked an elbow in her ribs. "Go on, you know you want 'im!"

She'd got Jean out in the lighted passage now, and gave her a pinch to make her get on and open the door, but Jean wouldn't. Madam Eva had to give her quite a sharp nip before she'd go in the kitchen, where Mr. Mitch was waiting for her.

She went in a few steps and stopped; she heard the door shut behind her. Mr. Mitch was sitting by the table. She'd never been alone in a room with him before.

He looked up at her. "My dear young lady," he said, his voice all soft. He was waiting for her to come over there to him.

Jean stood where she was; she couldn't have moved on or back, whatever you'd given her. She swayed a bit on her feet. Mr. Mitch jumped up and came over and took hold of her arm, to make her come and sit down in the chair. He was looking at her ever so hard, but she wouldn't look at him.

All at once she felt the blood rush up to her head, and the next thing she knew she was in the basket-chair with Madam Eva fussing over her, and Mr. Mitch sat down again over by the table, looking at her without so much as a word.

"Come over queer," Madam Eva was saying.

Jean didn't know where to look; she knew it was her she was talking about. "However could I be so silly."

"Never mind," Madam Eva told her. "All's well that ends well!"

She made Jean drink a cup of tea, and then she went back and sat at the table and talked over with Mr. Mitch when the wedding was to be, "And the sooner the better. Where's that dratted horoscope?"

He spread it out on the cloth, but she jerked it away from him, and they went on pulling it from one to the other, arguing over it.

"Well then, it ought to be the sixth."

"All right, make it the sixth, then. That's Monday week."

When they'd got that far Madam Eva folded up the paper and slapped it at him and told him he'd better get along now. "Can't you see the girl's done in?"

As soon as he'd gone she sent Jean off to bed. She lay there in the dark, staring out at the glimmer of rain on the iron roof across the yard. It wouldn't take a minute for her to go off so that Daisy could come. If only Daisy could tell her something for herself for once.

Whoever would have thought she'd fall in love with Mr. Mitch!

D

Madame Zinthia: Psychologist. A small brass plate beside the bell, in a row of polished bells. Sunshine lies along the other side of the street. There is little traffic; high-class tradesmen's vans are delivering at area gates. The houses are tall, grey, complacent.

Madame Zinthia consults in a small back room with draped window. The light filters dimly over black furniture. Madame Zinthia wears a black robe, cut medieval fashion, with long, hanging sleeves and a golden girdle. On a low, Oriental table the crystal lies on a black velvet cushion. Zinthia murmurs, in a throaty whisper, "Take it...in...your hand."

The crystal is large and cold.

"Hold it...so."

The crystal is heavy. A clock is ticking somewhere, Zinthia murmurs throatily, "Put it...on...the cushion."

She takes the cushion, with the crystal, on her knee and gazes at it abstractedly. In spite of yourself your heart is beating more rapidly than usual.

She says, on a deep, monotonous, tolling note, "I see...a cloud."

She pauses.

"A cloud...which hangs...over you. It hangs...over...your life. It is dark...and threatening."

She pauses. The clock ticks. The air is thick and sinister. The window must be tight shut behind the curtains. Your eyes are by now accustomed to the dim light. The Oriental table is a cheap imitation. The silence is ominous.

She gives a deep sigh, Ah-h-h.

"It will...lift. I see...far away...the glorious sun...breaking through. The clouds...will pass...away!"

She sinks back, exhausted. She is staring fixedly in front of her. After a long pause she sighs: "Is there...any...question...you would like to ask me?"

"I don't think.... That is..." Your voice, though you have spoken quietly, is loud and startling. It jars. Madame Zinthia shudders. You stop, appalled.

She waits. After a moment you whisper, "I suppose the cloud..." Your voice fails altogether.

Madame Zinthia looks neither to right nor left. She is gazing fixedly ahead. Her throaty, tolling note begins again: "It is...passing. It will roll away. The glorious sun...is breaking...through.

She stops. There is silence. She gives a deep sigh. Her eyes are covered.

You get up dazedly. "I think...your fee?"

You look around wildly. You drop the notes on the Oriental table and the coins on top. One of them rolls and tinkles against the brass. Zinthia shudders.

"Thank you," you mumble.

She is silent. Her head is drooped under her hand.

You claw at the door-handle through its hanging and get outside. Daylight hits you in the face. Without meaning to, you have slammed the door.

V

Jean was in a daze all that week before the wedding. There was Madam Eva fussing round over what clothes she ought to have, and should she be married from there or from home, and what ought she to wear to be married in? And Jean didn't know what to say about any of it.

Mr. Mitch said he wasn't going to have any fuss; they'd get married quiet at a registry, not Madam Eva's, and he didn't care what Jean had on. Only for *séances* afterwards she ought to have a long dress right down to the ground, blue it had to be, because blue was the colour of Venus. "My!" said Auntie Lil—she was coming round too, giving advice—"you don't think she's'a Venus, do you?"

Madam Eva explained it to her—how Venus was the sign Jean was born under, and Mr. Mitch was having the room done up blue for her with the signs of the Zodiac all round.—"My!"—Velvet, the dress had to be, blue velvet. "Fill her out," Madam Eva said; "she's so skinny." Mr. Mitch drew a picture of it, how it ought to be, and he said Madam Eva might as well get that if she wanted

89

to get something. The hardest thing Jean had to do that week was learn to call Mr. Mitch "Norman."

Norman didn't want a lot of fuss and people there, he said; he told Madam Eva he wanted to get it over quick and take Jean away home. "Go on," Madam Eva told him, "give the girl a chance. She'll only get married once."

"Let's 'ope so!" she went on, as an afterthought, and shook with laughing.

Norman laughed too, but he stuck to it, he didn't want a lot of people asked—only he couldn't help himself. There was Mum and Dad had to come, and Joyce, and Ted and his girl, and Norah with her Arnold she married six months back, and Doris and Auntie Lil, and then Mr. Harsett and Madam Eva. They had to put the kitchen-table in the front room.

When they'd all sat down Madam Eva suddenly let out a yell that there were thirteen of them, with Mr. Mitch and Jean, and someone would have to get up and go out. Everyone looked ever so uncomfortable and you could see Mum was worried to death, until Norman said it was all right, he was born on the fourth, and one and three makes four, so the thirteenth wasn't unlucky for him, though it might be for some people. So that made it all right, until Auntie Lil suddenly said, "But what about Jeannie?"

It was worse than ever then, everyone looking at Norman as if he'd done something awful. But he got up and made a lovely speech. "My dear friends," he said, "I think you've forgotten one visitor at this feast—an unseen guest: our little friend Daisy."

"Here-ere!" said Madam Eva. She was so pleased to have it cleared up that she dug Dad in the ribs with her elbow. "Just hark at 'im!" But Dad didn't take any notice of her.

Norman stood there and looked round. "I don't think anyone can doubt," he said, "that this little unseen visitor is looking down to-day and wishing luck to the bride as heartily as anyone here. There are therefore fourteen present, and the question does not arise."

When he sat down there was quite a clap round the table, especially from Ted and Norah's Arnold, who felt that as the only young fellows there they ought to have been the ones to offer to get up and go out. So everyone was happy then, and they all went on talking at once, and eating, and drinking healths, and Jean sat there in a daze; until Norman looked at his watch, and Madam Eva sent Mr. Harsett out for a taxi, and they all crowded round the top of the steps, where it was shivering cold after the heat in the front room, and watched Jean get in the taxi and drive off alone with Norman.

What with Daisy and Norman Jean was all in a daze. She was ever so fond of Norman, and it was as if Daisy knew all about it and was glad she and Norman had come there, where they could have *séances* and let Daisy talk. Sometimes when Norman had gone out to his studio on business and left

Jean alone in the back room she'd just sit down on a chair and drift off in a dream and start talking to Daisy. It was like having a friend to tell all about it to.

Norman had got her a lovely flat, up Baker Street way, with a lovely big front room to see clients in. It had two deep windows with long blue velvet curtains that would draw across, and the walls were all painted blue with the signs of the Zodiac all round in yellow, and the sun over the mantelpiece. And there wasn't any furniture except chairs put round the walls on three sides, and a big chair for Jean at the end, under the sun. It was lovely. They were going to have the first *séance* next Sunday. And then there was a little back room they lived in, and it had a gas-stove in the corner for Jean to cook on. When she'd got the room tidied up in the morning she pulled a screen across the middle of it, so that there was the bed on one side and the stove and the table they ate at on the other, and it was like having a little house.

Norman still kept on his studio up in the City, where he saw clients, and he went out in the morning at ten o'clock and came back at six. After he'd gone out Jean tidied up the room in a dreamy sort of way and did the shopping, and then she used to go in to dust the chairs in the front room and stand there staring up at the paintings on the walls, thinking how lovely it was. Once when she was waiting for Norman to come and he was a bit late, all at once she felt quite faint with listening for him, and she sat down on one of the chairs, with the duster in her hand, and almost before she'd sat she could hear Daisy's voice. "Here I am!" she said. And Jean didn't know any more until she came back, and Norman was there, putting his arm round her ever so softly, going to lift her up; and she fainted right off again she was so happy.

Daisy was coming ever so much more often here than at Madam Eva's. Jean'd only got to shut her eyes for it to go dark and Daisy to start talking. She wasn't even afraid about the *séance*, though Norman said there'd be ever so many there, real top-notchers.

Sunday afternoon, when she'd cleared away the dinner, she put on the blue velvet dress Norman had designed and Madam Eva gave her for a wedding-present. It came right down to the floor. It seemed ever so funny swishing round in long skirts among the crowded-up furniture; she hoped she wouldn't get any grease on it from the stove. Norman was busy putting himself into his velvet coat and sleeking brilliantine on his hair; he had to show the people in and introduce her when they were all ready. She wasn't to come in until he told her, when everyone was there, and not speak to them, only go to her chair and settle herself and go off. He was busy tying up his tie in a bow. He said she'd have to learn to talk properly now, in a more refined way, not dropping her aitches like Madam Eva did, now she'd got a real high-class connexion. But it didn't matter for now, because it would only be Daisy's voice speaking. He was going to introduce her as "Madam Jan," he said—which was French—because it sounded better.

The bell started going, and he went down to show people up into the front room. Jean sat down on a chair and waited, not to get her frock dirty. Her eyes felt ever so heavy, but she was afraid to shut them for fear of going off before Norman came to fetch her.

When he fetched her in she saw he had drawn the curtains and made it quite dark, though it was the middle of the day. There was only one little light lit, behind the big empty chair where she had to sit. All the other chairs were pulled out away from the wall in a half-circle, and full of ladies and gentlemen. And there were twenty of them; she knew that because she'd counted the chairs.

She went up to the end and sat down and shut her eyes, and it all started going round. Norman was standing behind her shoulder. She heard him say, "Ladies and gentlemen." And they all stopped coughing and whispering. "I have pleasure in introducing this remarkable trance medium, Madam Jan, of whom you have all heard. You will now have the opportunity…"

And then she heard Daisy speak up, "Hallo, everybody, here I am!"

When she came round some of them were whispering among themselves, but very polite and quiet, not like them at Madam Eva's. When they saw Jean's eyes were open and she was sitting looking at them without saying anything they all stopped talking.

Then Norman took hold of her arm and whispered to her to get up and come out of the room. As soon as she was outside he went back; he didn't draw the curtains, but put the lights on—she heard him—and they all started talking out loud, polite company talk, and went away downstairs.

Norman was ever so pleased with the way it had gone off. He said all those people would go away and tell others, and they'd have *séances* twice a week, Wednesdays as well as Sundays.

Jean was glad, because Daisy must be pleased too. She asked Norman that—whether Daisy'd said anything; and he told her, yes; it was just what Daisy wanted.

He was undoing his tie in front of the glass. Jean came up and stood by him and said, "I'm ever so glad, Norman." She still felt shy of him in a way.

Norman stayed at home from his studio on Wednesdays after that; they had the *séance* twice a week. And then ladies and gentlemen who'd been to it began to ring up for private sittings. The first time it happened it was one morning just after Norman had gone out, and Jean didn't know what to say. She said, yes, the lady could come; and then she went and pulled two chairs together in a corner of the big room, it seemed so funny having just one lady in it, and saw her in her ordinary clothes, in the daylight. It seemed so silly dressing up just for one.

It was an elderly lady, ever so kind. When Jean came back from her trance she told her, "You're very young to be doing this." But quite nice—not like they used to be, grumbling.

"Only you didn't bring me exactly anybody I know," she said. "Only a little girl—quite a dear little girl. She told me a great deal about life in the beautiful world beyond the grave."

"Oh, dear," Jean told her, "I am sorry! Didn't she bring anyone you knew?"

There now, of course it was her husband she wanted to talk to. Whatever was Daisy thinking about?

"I'm ever so sorry, reely I am. That was Daisy, the little girl you 'eard...you heard," she said, remembering. "She's my guide you know. She doesn't often do a thing like that."

But the lady said it didn't matter at all, and perhaps Daisy would bring someone to talk to her another day. And then she said, "Now what do I owe you?

Jean didn't know what to say; she charged her a guinea, the same Madam Eva used to for the crystal.

But when Norman came back and she told him he was ever so annoyed; he said it ought to have been five at least for a private sitting, and Jean must never let anyone see her except in the special dress, and when it was worn out they'd get another. And she had to have the room and the lighting fixed up properly too, even for one lady. He said now he saw it was taking on he'd give up his own business and stay at home and manage for her.

Jean told him then how the lady had said Daisy didn't bring anyone, but only talked herself. And he said that was for Jean to see to; she ought to have concentrated on it before she went off.

So the next time a lady came Jean looked at her and tried ever so hard to see what she wanted. She could tell there was something worrying her, and then all at once when the lady sat down it was as if there was something behind her shoulder for a minute, like a little girl's head with curly hair. So she whispered to Daisy in her mind, "It's another little girl; do bring her, Daisy." And Daisy must have, because the lady didn't complain.

After that Norman didn't go to his studio anymore. He used to answer the telephone and make appointments. And when anyone was coming he answered the door and brought them upstairs, and then Jean just went in in her blue dress and sat down without saying anything and went off. Just before she got right off she'd nearly always hear Daisy say, "Hallo, everybody, here I am!" And afterwards Norman came in and settled money, while Jean slipped away into the back room.

Once Norman told her Daisy oughtn't to "Hallo, everybody," when there was only one sitter there.

That puzzled Jean too. "I don't know what she does that for."

Next time she heard Daisy start, "Hallo," she thought, "She oughtn't to say 'everybody' and it brought her right back. She didn't know what to do for a minute. She opened her eyes and looked at the sitter, who was a gentleman, and he looked quite surprised; and Jean could feel herself going in a sweat with fear, the way she used to when she started. Then she shut her eyes, and after a minute Daisy started again, "Hallo, everybody!" and she went off all right.

When she told Norman about bothered for a minute, and asked her if she felt she wanted a rest. Which gave her quite a surprise—"Why, whatever would that do?"

Norman looked at her, and then he told her all right; let Daisy say whatever she wanted and not try to interrupt her another time, she didn't like it.

Jean was quite nervous what Daisy next time if she was cross with her, but Daisy started off the same as ever; and it went off all right, and Norman looked relieved. In between letting in clients he used to sit at the table in the back room and do astrological work by post; he didn't want to lose his connexion, he said.

Once when Madam Eva dropped in to see them she asked him what he did it for, seeing they were doing so well with the *séances* and the rest.

He told her, "My dear lady, no craze goes on forever." Jean wondered whatever he meant. Then he went on to say he was thinking of a plan to hire a big public hall for Jean that would hold hundreds of people, and have a big public meeting with Daisy talking. She could make a speech, he said, and give messages afterwards.

"Make hay while the sun shines, eh?"

But he changed his mind about it. He said after all Daisy's voice would never carry in a big hall, and it was better to keep it exclusive, the way it was.

It seemed as if everyone wanted to hear Daisy now, and some days Jean would have two appointments running. It was dreadful tiring. Dreadfully, she ought to say. But Daisy was always ready to talk, which was a blessing, and generally she'd bring along the person they wanted. Very often Jean would see something when she first came in the room, such as someone looking over their shoulder that was waiting to talk, or else it might just flash through her mind when she looked at them what it was that was bothering them, and then she'd tell Daisy to be sure and remember.

Now that she was used to it she liked the *séance*; best, when there was a lot of people there; it was easier than with only the one client. You could feel them all there waiting, wanting to be helped, and it seemed to come out to you. Daisy liked it too; she liked helping a lot of people, and she'd be sure to get some of them right. And then, too, when it was a proper *séance* with a lot there Norman always came in with her and stood by her all the time, and Daisy liked that; she'd always do it better in a way with Norman there.

Very often when Jean came in and up the room past them in the half-dark she could feel at once who were the ones who wanted helping. You could tell half the time the ones that only came out of curiosity, seeing if you could do it. Inquirers, they called them. It put Daisy off if there were too many there thinking nasty. Sometimes Norman would know some of the real ones that had been there before and tell her about them when he came to fetch her. "There's Mrs. Muffle there again. She didn't get a message last time, poor old thing." And then just before Jean went right off she'd ask Daisy, special, to try if she couldn't say something for Mrs. Muffle.

And afterwards, generally, he'd tell her, "Well, you got her all right to-day."

Once when he came for her he said, "Mind there's old Mrs. Smith there; she hasn't had a message the last three times."

"All right," she whispered. She went in and up the room to her chair, standing alone under the half-seen yellow sun, with Norman behind her, and they all moved their heads to look at her as she went by. The curtains were drawn and only the little light was on, behind her empty chair, shining on their faces, so that she could make out some, a few that had been there before. Old Mrs. Smith sitting at the end, with her fur coat and pearl necklace, and Norman said she'd lost her son, poor thing, back in the War, and she'd got some lovely messages from him sometimes. And one of the men too—she couldn't remember his name— he was something big in business and lost his son in a motor accident. And a young woman in black, whose husband drowned himself. She knew all that from what Norman told her. And then there were some she didn't know; she only had time to notice a few: quite a young girl in country tweeds, and a pale young man.

Then she sat down and they were all looking at her, and she shut her eyes and thought about Daisy till she was there clear in front of her. "Let Mrs. Smith get a message; there's a dear."

She heard Norman's voice going on, fading off in the distance. "You will now hear her spirit-guide, the little girl Daisy who passed over more than twenty years ago, but in the ageless world of spirits remains at the age at which she left this earth, and has come here to-day, ready and eager to help your dear ones speak with you."

Daisy was coming up closer, big and misty, and all at once nearer and nearer at a rush. But her voice was small, from a long way off, right away down the end of a tunnel...small and clear: "Hallo, everybody, here I am!"

Madame Jeanne, dark, sweeping skirts draped around her feet, was seated in a high-backed chair facing the semi-circle. Her head was leaning against the back of the chair and her eyes were shut; she might have been asleep. Her face was in shadow. She was speaking in a little girl's voice; "Hallo, everybody, there's lots an' lots of people wants to talk to you to-day! They all keep on coming round. One of them keeps saying, 'Can't I talk to Dad?' And there's another one—no, you can't, then; go on! He keeps saying, 'Let me talk, Daisy; go on, do.' You go on; you wait your turn!"

They sat in a dark, uneven semi-circle, watching Madame Jeanne. She was motionless, the high child's voice coming shrill and exclamatory from her mouth. A rather stout, middle-aged man with sleeked-down hair and a pasty face and a brown velvet jacket was standing at her shoulder.

Professor Norman Mitch. I suppose he's her husband.

Oh dear, I wonder if anything will come through. Why does the man stand so close to her? Might be ventriloquism? Her lips are obviously moving, though.

"I say, here's Donald, he wants to speak to his Dad!"

A grey-haired man shifted in his chair. One or two people glanced round and then away again. He said nervously, clearing his throat, "That you, Donald?"

"Hallo, Dad, this is Donald. How's Mother? Why doesn't she come too?"

...Or hypnosis, of course. Only how does he know, any more than she does?

"Mother couldn't come. You know how it is, don't you, Donald? But you know what a comfort your messages are to me."

"I say, Dad, you tell Mother she must come too; you tell..."

Then Daisy: "Here's another one, it's a lady. She says she wants David!"

The pale young man shifted in an embarrassed way. "Yes, Mother?"

They looked away, staring in the half-light at the medium.

They call her Madame, but she looks quite a young girl. Sweet-natured—but so tired. She looks very sweet in that dress. They say she's wonderful; Jane said so. She said she was wonderful with her.

Hoodlum. And why do they have to dress up. I don't know, though; there might be something.

I wonder why this little girl Daisy can make it easier for Donald to come back?

"Are you happy, Mother?"

"Very, very happy, my son."

How does she get the different voices? Rather clever, really.

"I'm always thinking of you, Mother."

The girl in the tweeds was nervously clenching her hands. Perhaps Tony doesn't want to talk—or can't the woman do it? Perhaps he doesn't like my coming here; he always rather hated that sort of thing. I do wish he'd come, and then I could ask him. I wonder who the man is, and why he stands there all the time.

"I say, here's Jackie now; he wants his Mummy!"

A middle-aged woman jerked out, "Jackie! My own little Jackie!"

"Mum, Mum!"

"Tell Mummy all about it, darling. What's it like over there?"

I do wish they'd hurry up. Mother will never believe I've been all this time at Elizabeth's. I do think there can't be anything in it, or Tony would say something. I suppose they don't always talk to everybody, though. There must be something in it or people wouldn't keep on coming.

Why doesn't she get Rupert? I know he wants to speak to me. That's three times—four with to-day. He doesn't like coming here. I expect he doesn't like that little girl Daisy; she's a silly little thing. I'll try another one; I'll try that one they were talking about at Mrs.... I wonder if Norman Mitch is really her husband—or, of course, you never know with these people.... I really don't think she's any good....

"Oh, it's lovely, Mummy; it's lovely! It's all full of lovely wab-bits an' little chickens, and I've got a puppy to play with, just like R-R-Rex, and..."

"Oh, Jackie, then you do remember Rex?"

"Yes, rather, Mummy."

"Jackie, my own little Jackie! Then I'm sure it really is you."

How is it that when they do get something right it's nearly always something so trivial...?

"And there's lots an' lots of puppies, all the little boys has got puppies, and..."

Daisy's voice: "Here's another, people! He won't say what his name is, he's quite a young chap. I say, he says his name's R-R-R..."

"Richard!" The young woman in black, who had sat all the time in frozen silence, suddenly came to life. "So you did, after all."

Mrs. Smith sat up, firmly clutching her handbag. "Rupert! I knew you'd come and speak to Mother. Why didn't you talk before?

Don't you like coming here? Speak to me, Rupert."

"Oh, please don't interrupt."

Mrs. Smith looked round glassily. "Would you very kindly…"

The middle-aged woman whose turn was over was wiping her eyes. It's lovely. It's well worth it. It's worth anything. I must try to manage another time.

"Richard! Are you still there?"

"Why don't you say something, Rupert?"

A voice from the end exclaimed impatiently, "Well, which is he?"

Oh, do you think it was Tony? But he'd say so if it was. I'm sure he doesn't like my coming.

"Why won't you let him talk? Why won't you?"

Daisy's voice: "Oh, I say, people, he's gone away, he said he'll come another time."

"It was my son Rupert. Why can't you get him?"

Daisy's voice, excitedly: "I say, here's another—no, he's gone away. There's such a lot! I say… "

Professor Norman Mitch stepped forward. "Ladies and gentlemen, the medium is now passing out of the trance state. There will be no further messages at this sitting."

He switched on the ceiling lights. Madame Jeanne shivered convulsively, opened her eyes and stared at them.

Norman was ever so cross when they'd all gone. "You never got Mrs. Smith's again," he said. "What's the idea? D'you think people are coming here week after week for nothing? I tipped you off about her before you went in, didn't I? What were you thinking of? And then making all that mess at the end."

Jean was sitting on the chair in the back room; she was tired right out. She just stared at Norman.

He came over and shook her by the shoulder. "What's the idea, letting the whole thing down? After all I've spent on getting you started."

Jean began to cry. "I'm ever so sorry, Norman. I did ask Daisy, special, to say something for Mrs. Smith, but I can't make her do it if she doesn't want to. Sometimes she will and sometimes she won't."

Norman said, "Psh!" You could see he was furious. He was taking off his velvet jacket, hanging it up behind the curtain on the wall. He said, "That's enough of your precious Daisy. It's time you got on and did a job of work if you don't want to lose this connexion, after all the trouble I've had building it up."

Jean went on crying. She only said, "Oh, Norman." She didn't know which she was crying for—Norman being so cross, or him being nasty about Daisy.

He took his coat down from the door and put it on.

"Oh, Norman, you aren't going out, are you?" He didn't say anything until he'd found his hat and gloves, and then he only said, giving her a cold look, "You'd better lie down. I shan't be in till late."

"Oh, Norman!"

But he'd shut the door by then.

Jean sat and cried. She couldn't make it out, why Norman was nasty to her all at once.

After she'd cried a bit she got up, sniffing, and took the blue frock off and folded it carefully away in the drawer and put on her old skirt and cardigan.

She went in mechanically to clear up the big room. It was all in the dark; Norman had put the lights out without opening the curtains. She drew them back and saw it was getting dark now outside.

In the dusk she started putting the chairs straight. She was so tired she didn't know what to do. She went backwards and forwards across the big room, taking a chair from the broken semi-circle and carrying it back to stand under a yellow painting on the darkening blue wall. When she'd moved half of them she sat down on the next and put her elbows on her knees and her head in her hands.

If only Daisy would help her out. Whatever was she going to do if Daisy stopped helping her? Suppose Daisy got cross with Norman being nasty about her and wouldn't come anymore, whatever would Norman say then? Oh, do help me, Daisy, there's a dear. Don't go, will you; I don't know whatever I'd do. Don't take any notice of him, 'e doesn't mean it. Do help me to do what he wants, there's a good girl, and speak nice and keep up his 'igh-class connexion. And don't let me down, will you Daisy, say you won't.

And all at once Daisy said, clear as clear, "Hallo everybody, here I am!"

It was the telephone bell that brought her back. She sat up with a start. It was such a wonderful feeling, as if Daisy'd been talking with her in her mind.

The bell went on ringing outside the door. The room was pitch dark now. She felt her way across, feeling in the emptiness for the door ahead, and switched on the light outside. A lady's voice, said, "Can I make an appointment with Madame Jeanne?"

Jean was so full of Daisy and how lovely it was talking with her all by herself that before she knew what she was doing she said, "I'm sorry, Madam Jan's out just now."

"Oh," said the lady, "then I'll ring up another time."

When she'd put down the 'phone she felt dreadful. Telling a lie like that!... She didn't know when she'd ever done such a thing.

But she was so pleased about Daisy she didn't worry over it very long. She said to Daisy, in her mind, You don't care, do you? She'll ring again; she said she would.

And she could hear Daisy answer back clear as clear not out loud, like when she really went off; it was only in her mind, but ever so clear—That's all right, Jee-een!

She switched on the lights then in the big room, and put all the chairs straight. She didn't know whether to cook any supper, whether Norman was coming in. He didn't—not until it got late; and then he wouldn't speak to her. It made her ever so sad.

Next day he didn't say any more about Daisy, though. But he still didn't take any notice of Jean. It was as if he felt ashamed of himself in a way.

Then the lady rang up again and came for a private sitting; and it must have gone off all right because Norman cheered up after that, especially when there were more appointments going on the same as usual. Before the next *séance* she did wonder if Mrs. Smith was coming again, and Norman didn't say anything; so at last she asked him when he came to fetch her. She hardly dared to. "Norman," she said, not daring to look at him hardly, "is Mrs. Smith in there?"

"No," he said. "She isn't."

You could tell he was annoyed, but he didn't say any more. And the *séance* went off all right, cause he whistled afterwards, while he was taking off his velvet coat, between his teeth—the way he only did when he was pleased about something.

Jean slipped out of her frock, and stood there a minute, waiting for him to take notice of her, but he only went on whistling.

"Norman," she said, and she went over and stood by him. He was in his shirt-sleeves, going to take his coat down from the door—the old coat he did his work in. "Norman, you aren't cross with me anymore, are you?"

He looked round at her sharp, and then after a minute he gave one of his slow smiles. He put his coat back on the peg and sat down and took her on his knee.

Daisy was lovely to her now; she always said what she ought to, and ladies and gentlemen kept on coming, and then Norman was nice.

Sometimes if he was out Jean would stand and look out of the window in the back room, over the bit of ground-floor garden into the gardens of the houses behind, and talk to Daisy, and ask her to go on like she was and not let Jean let Norman down anymore. And she got to hear Daisy answer, quite plain, whenever she spoke to her. That's all right, Jee-een, she'd say. You go on; that's all right. And Jean would say, Daisy lovey, you are a dear.

But then she started being sick at night, every few nights, and everything went wrong again. Norman got cross because he couldn't get his sleep, and Jean was so tired out next day she was all listless and stupid and appointments began to drop off. And when Norman found out she was going to have a baby it was worse than anything.

Jean was pleased at first; she thought it would be nice to have a dear little baby, if only it wouldn't make her feel so sick and weak. But Norman was wild about it. He said did she imagine you could keep a baby in a flat that size, and what was going to happen to the connexion all the time she wasn't any good? "It's too bad," he said. "After I've gone and spent everything on getting the place fixed up for you."

He said he supposed he'd have to set up on his own again, to tide them over.

Jean was ever so unhappy. She'd wake up in the early morning and hear Norman swear and turn over when she got out of bed. It was hardly light, and she'd stand there being sick over the sink and shivering with sickness and cold. When she got back in she'd say, "Norman, I'm ever so sorry." But he only swore at her and turned his back.

Poor Norman, it was awful for him; he got fed up. One morning when a lady came who'd got an appointment Jean was too bad to see her, and Norman had to go in and apologize. She heard him putting it as nice as he could: "I very much regret, my dear madam..."

When he came back Jean said—she felt awful— P'raps she'll come back another time."

"So likely," he said. "D'you suppose she's going to stand on the doorstep till you feel like seeing her?"

Jean didn't know what to do. They had the *séance* the same as usual. But when she was going out of the room afterwards she heard someone say, "How ill she looks!" And Norman heard it too; he was wild.

Daisy came all right, but she wouldn't stay very long. Sometimes there were long silences, Norman said, in between messages, and it made people feel they weren't getting their money's worth. And Jean would come round, feeling faint and giddy, hardly able to get out of the room. After a few weeks people began to drop off.

When Madam Eva came Norman told her about it. "It's sickening," he said. "Sickening."

Madam Eva took one look at Jean: You don't need to tell me." She asked Jean, "Why didn't you tell me before? I might've done something for you."

"Anyhow," she told Norman, what's the hoot about business falling off? I 'ad my Elsie, and saw clients right up to the last."

"My dear lady," he said, "*you* had some sense."

He went on about how silly Jean was, and how she would go on about Daisy would do it or Daisy wouldn't; and Jean began to cry, looking at her.

Madam Eva pulled him up short: "The girl's anaemic, she always was. What she wants is feeding up and see the doctor."

Norman said with someone temperamental like Jean was he wondered whether to shut up shop a together, advertise that she'd gone away for a bit, instead of getting everyone fed up—and then stage a come-back for her afterwards. He said it was a dead loss, but not worse than losing all the connexion through her tantrums.

Jean cried then, but Madam Eva said he might be right.

So Norman took a studio again, where he could carry on his own business, and was out all day from ten in the morning. Sometimes he didn't get in till late at night. He wasn't nasty to her, but he had the look all the time that she'd let him down, and it made her ever so depressed.

Madam Eva came in sometimes in the evenings, and showed her how to sew baby clothes, and made sure she had her tea properly.

Jean wondered how Madam Eva was getting on all by herself, and she said, "The same as ever."

It must be wonderful being able to go on the same year after year like Madam Eva.

Madam Eva told her she hadn't any business being depressed, she ought to be glad to think she was going to give a home to some little spirit that was wandering round homeless. And she ought to be thinking what sort of a spirit she wanted to draw to her. If she wanted it psychic she ought to *think* psychic.

Jean had never thought about it like that. But after this, when she was alone, she used to sit and look out over the back, where you could see a bit of a tree with leaves on, in between the houses, and think what sort of a baby she wanted. Curly-haired and good as gold, and lovely-looking when she grew up. She'd like best for it to be a little girl. And then she asked Daisy to bring along a lovely spirit that would be psychic and go on helping people the way Daisy did.

She was talking a lot to Daisy now; she was afraid Daisy wouldn't like it not having people coming there for her to talk to. Go on, she used to say, talk to me instead, do Daisy. Talk so that I can hear you. Do tell me what sort of a baby I'll have, and if Norman'll be glad, and if he'll be nice again like he was before.

She used to go about doing her work, making the bed and washing up, talking to Daisy all the time. Go on, she'd say, do tell me what my little baby'll be like. Will I have a little girl?

And once she heard Daisy say, clear as clear, That's right, Jeeeen! A lovely little girl!

She was ever so pleased then. She used to get on with her work, talking to Daisy about what her little girl was going to be like. After Norman went out in the morning she used to tidy the place as soon as she felt up to it, and wash up the things in the sink, and then go out down to the shops to buy what was needed. Once when she was in a shop a lady came in with a little girl, ever so pretty, with short, curly hair and pink cheeks. The lady sat her down on a chair by the counter, and Jean couldn't help looking at her while she waited her turn.

The little girl saw her looking and looked too, and presently she gave her a smile. The assistant came just then, and Jean had to turn round and ask for what she wanted. She heard the little girl say, "Oh, Mummy, look at the lady!" And it made her ever so happy. Do give me a dear little girl like that one Daisy, there's a love, do.

When she got home and upstairs with her shopping she had to rest for a bit; it tired her out, with the hot weather coming on. But then in the afternoon she got out her sewing and sat down at the table with it and went on making little clothes the way Madam Eva showed her. She was ever so slow at it, and the needle kept on pricking her finger. She couldn't help thinking about the little girl in the shop, and how she was a bit like Daisy to look at. Will I have a little girl that looks like you, Daisy? I do hope I will. Wouldn't it be lovely? It'd be like having you living here where I could see you all the time. But I wouldn't talk to her instead of you—you know I wouldn't; so you wouldn't mind, would you? You don't *mind* me having a little girl, do you, Daisy? You know I wouldn't think more of her than I do of you. It's only that I'd like to have her look like you, ever so much.

Then all at once she stuck the needle hard in her finger, and never felt it, because she'd only just thought, Oo, Daisy! Oo, Daisy, it wouldn't truly be *you*, would it?

She never thought of that before! Suppose it reely-truly was Daisy. Wouldn't it be lovely? Having Daisy to talk to, reely there all the time.

She couldn't go on with her sewing after that. She just put it down in front of her and sat with her hands in her lap, thinking how lovely it would be having Daisy there, with her yellow curls, calling her Mum—Oo, Daisy, you wouldn't, would you? —wouldn't it be funny? And hearing her little voice laughing, cheering up the place; she was always such a cheery little thing. And when she got a bit older, going to school. Coming home up the stairs, saying, "Hallo, Mum, here I am!" She could hear her say it now. Oo, Daisy, did you reely say it? Are you reely going to come? Do say, go on.

But Daisy wouldn't tell her for sure; she was teasing.

It made Jean ever so happy. Even when she had to get up to be sick she didn't mind so much, thinking it might be Daisy she was doing it for.

And when Norman had gone out and she was dragging round getting her work done, so tired and washed out she didn't know what to do hardly, it would make her smile all at once to fancy she could see Daisy there like she'd be some day, hopping round, with her cheery little face, wiping the dishes while Jean washed. You'd help me, wouldn't you, lovey? You'd help Mum?

And then she'd think how she was ungrateful, seeing how Daisy came to talk to her now when she might be off playing with all the other little girls and boys that had passed over in the lovely spirit-world. Oo, Daisy, I didn't mean it! You do help me now, lovey—ever so much. Only I do feel bad, reely I do.

And then when she turned round and saw the room, with the bed not made yet because it fagged her so to do it, and the faded old curtain on the wall, bulging out with Norman's clothes, and the table that wanted a good scrub down, she couldn't help thinking Daisy'd never choose a home like that when she had all there was to choose from. You didn't ought to, lovey, reely you didn't. I never ought to ask you. You ought to pick a lovely home with some rich lady for your Mummy, and a garden to run in and toys to play with. You never would want to come here, would you, lovey? Only I would be ever so fond of you; I'd do anything to make it nice like you wanted. I'd work my fingers to the bone, reely I would. No rich lady couldn't be half so fond of you as me. And then she sat down on the unmade bed and cried.

When she felt a bit better she wiped her eyes and went in to dust the chairs in the big room. Daisy's room, she always called it.

P'raps Norman would let her play about in here, and then she'd feel more at home.

Sometimes she thought she'd like to sit in there with her sewing, but she never did; it would be too much like sewing in church. She only went in every day and drew back the lovely heavy velvet curtains and dusted the chairs standing all round the wall and swept over the big, empty polished floor that was like a ball-room. Sometimes when she'd finished she sat down on one of the chairs and put her hands in her lap and waited for Daisy to come to her. When she went right off she never knew what Daisy said—only when she came back she knew Daisy'd been there, and it gave her a lovely happy, friendly feeling. Then she drew the curtains again across the windows, and left the room dark and clean and empty, ready for when it was all over and people came again for Daisy to talk to.

It was one day when she'd drawn the curtains and gone across in the dark to the door and had her hand on the knob that she suddenly thought, if Daisy comes, if Daisy's my little girl, here on earth, then she won't be able to talk anymore. Will she?

It made her go weak all over. She felt her way along the wall to the nearest chair and sat down. Oo Daisy, do tell me, do tell me. What'm I to do? Daisy, do tell me.

Presently Daisy said, Here I am, Jee-een!

Oo Daisy, do tell me. Will my little girl be you? And if you are her will you be able to talk like you do now? Because I couldn't do the *séances* without you, could I, Daisy? Or would you send some-one else to do it? Would you send another spirit and you come and be my little girl?—or don't you want to be, Daisy, do tell me.

Jee-een! Here I am!

Oh dear, what do you mean, I do wish you'd say. Do you mean here you are, staying and being a spirit talking to people, or do you mean here you are coming... Oo Daisy, do tell me what I ought to do if you're my little girl and you can't talk to me anymore.

But Daisy only said, Jee-een!

She wouldn't say any more. P'raps she can't, I do wonder. P'raps they won't let them say. P'raps…

But Norman came in then, and Jean had to feel her way out and get his tea.

He hung his coat up on the door and pulled on the old jacket he wore in the house. "Hurry along with it," he said. "I've got work to do."

As soon as the table was cleared he got out his books and papers from his attaché case and spread them over the table and started drawing up an astrological chart.

Jean washed up the tea things and went and sat over by the sink to be out of his way, with her sewing. It did puzzle her about Daisy. P'raps it meant Daisy didn't want to stop being a spirit and be a little girl again, only she didn't like to say so, in case Jean minded. She told her, Never mind, lovey, if you don't want to. You go on talking to me like you do now, and send me some little girl that's a friend of yours. Only I would, truly, like it to be you.

She pricked herself, and sewed and watched Norman working at the table, over under the light. You know I would; don't you, Daisy?

Once when he came to the end of something and looked up she said all at once, "Norman?"

"Well, what?"

"Couldn't you do a horoscope to find out what my baby'll be like?"

He shrugged his shoulders impatiently. "How d'you think I can cast a horoscope without the date and time of birth."

"I'm sorry, Norman."

He went on with his work.

Date and time of birth. How funny. She hadn't really thought about baby really having to be born. It wasn't very long now, either. It was going to be a summer baby—August. Madam Eva said she ought to go into hospital for it, only Jean would really rather it was here, where Daisy knew the place—in case she couldn't find her way, if Jean went somewhere else, in case she really did mean to come. Oo do tell me, lovey, I won't mind, reely I won't. Only do tell me if it's you to not.

It puzzled her so she even said it to Norman once, one day when it was getting quite near the time. It was a morning, when he was getting ready to go out, and she was sitting there trying to get up her strength to dress herself and tidy up. And it was ever so hot—it was hot summer; it got her right down. She watched him brush round his hat and pick up his gloves, and then when he was going for his rolled-up umbrella that he always carried, natty-looking, she asked him, "Norman?"

"Well?"

"Norman, I do wonder sometimes, do you think Daisy might want to stop being a spirit and come and be a little girl again? Do you think she might come and be my baby?"

Norman gave a laugh; she hadn't heard him laugh for months past.

He'd got his umbrella from the corner and hung on his arm by now. "Well, what is it? I'm in a hurry."

"Oo, Norman, if Daisy came and was my little girl she couldn't be a spirit too and go on talking could she? And I do wonder, do you think she'd rather go on talking to people when we have the *séances* again?"

Norman said, "Psh! Now if that's all you've got to say I've something else to do."

Then when he'd got the door open he turned round and said, "The public's fed up with your Daisy, anyhow. That's played out. You'd better use your time thinking up something fresh."

E

Madam Bertha sits at her table and pants. She has just run in along the passage that leads from the street, beside the photographer's.
"Sorry to keep you waitin'. Just 'ad to run out a minute."

The table is too small for Madam Bertha—so is the chair. Its back disappears behind her massive shoulders. Two little shaggy dogs in flannel coats have woken from their sleep in two basket-chairs by the gas-fire and are yapping at one another. Madam Bertha is big and blonde and blowsy. She begins to shuffle among the untidy papers on the table. "What was it you wanted? Full readin'? 'And? Astrologic?" *She pushes out a toe at one of the dogs.* "Keep quiet, can't you!"

The dog makes a run at her foot; so does the other. They both yap.
"Now what I'd advise you… Keep quiet, can't you?"

She sits up and bellows, "Ethel! Doris! Isn't any of you there! Ethel!"

"Aw?" *says a voice outside the door.*

"Come 'ere! Take these dawgs out, can't you!"

An untidy girl in a coat and no hat pushes her head round the door. "Eh?"

"Take these dawgs out!"

Ethel gapes.

"DAWGS!"

They are bounding about the small room, yapping and worrying. Ethel sees them. She makes a dab at one and misses it. They yap and run away. She chases them, knocking over a chair. She picks up a dog and drops it. She gets them both outside, and the door is shut again.

"And stay out!"

Madam Bertha leans back and puffs. "Be the deather me woner these days!"

She sits up and shuffles the papers. "Now what I was sayin'.... I'd advise you to 'ave the full read in'. Much most satisfactory. 'And an' astrologic—gives the bes' results. Full pycherlogic readin'." She fishes out a piece of blank paper from among the scattered piles. "Now you jus' tell me date'n placer birth, name'n age."

She starts writing laboriously, interspacing the words with astrological signs, talking continuously in a soothing confidential patter: "Now don't you worry; you'll be pleased with it, I know you will. And I wouldn't tell you that if I didn't know you will, mind. Well, I'll tell you what I'll do, seein' you're takin' the two, 'and an astrologic—I'll do you the lot for thirty bob! Now that's a real bargain, mind. That's right. An' you'll be pleased; I know you will.

"Now jus' you give me somethin' to old what you're wearin'; watch'll do. That's right; I shan't 'urt it. Jus' let me get the feel of it."

She closes her left hand over the watch. Her right goes on covering the paper with laboured signs.

"That's right. Now the feelin' I get with this... What I get is the feelin' of someone doesn't know where they're goin' to."

She waits.

"Jus' let me see yer 'and. That's right, that's jus' what I was sayin'. An' it's the same 'ere..." Her pencil taps the paper. "The same as the feelin' what I get—as if it was someone doesn't know where they're goin'.

"Now as I was sayin'..."

"Aw?" Ethel pokes her head round the door.

"What is it now? What d'you want? What did I tell you."

"It's the men-ew?" She holds it out.

"Eh? 'Ere, give it 'ere."

Madam Bertha snatches the card, leans back and studies it with close interest. "I'll 'ave, let me see... I'll take the chop 'n peas, mashed, apple tart, cheese 'n coffee." She closes her eyes momentarily, gives a sigh of repletion, jerks back the card. "'Ere. Now you get out.

"Well, now, as I was sayin'..."

She goes on making signs on the paper. She has forgotten the watch; it is half buried under the pushed-about rubbish on the table. "An' you won't live to be a burden to anyone." She sighs heavily, closing her yes. "Never will live to be a burden."

Presently she catches a glance towards the watch, pushes it absently across the table and struggles with decision to her feet. "Now you wait till you get the full readin'. Will you call for it or will I post it? Let me see, 'ave I got your address? Oh, all right then; you'll call. It'll take some time, mind; it's gotter be all wrote out. An' I 'aven't been at all well lately; got be'ind somethin' terrible. 'Ad a terrible lotter trouble with me jaw. 'Ad to 'ave it cut right open."

She strokes it and stares reminiscently. "Blood-pois'nin', that's what it was. Goin' all over me body. Well, as I was sayin', look at all this lot I got waitin' now." She shuffles over the piles. "That's right, readin's, everyone of 'em. But don't you worry, you shall 'ave it; I never disappoint. There was one we sent out this very mornin' was ordered for a doctor gentleman; you can see for yerself... Ethel!

"You there! Ethel! Where the 'ell...!"

"Aw?"

"Where's the register slip for that readin' we sent out the smornin' for Dr Blumminy?"

"Eh?"

"Where's the register slip?"

"Dunno-o."

"*All right. Get out! Well, there was that one this very mornin', an' all this lot I've got be'ind…. But you shall 'ave it; don't you worry.*

"*Eh? Who's that out there? 'Oo is it? Eh? That you, Lulu? Don't go; I've done!*

"*Well, you jus' come back in a bit 'n you shall 'ave it.*

"*'Ere, don't go; I wanter see yer!*

"*Come in any time you like, that's right; 'n you shall 'ave it if it's ready. Bye-bye!*"

VI

So, after all, baby was born in hospital. They got the ambulance, someone did, and Jean was ever so ill, and she was away there in the hospital. Daisy kept coming saying Here I am, Jee-een!— And Norman, looking all funny, someone got him, what did they get him for, he was ever so nasty over Daisy. Daisy lovey, do come, don't mind him, what did they get him there for, and Daisy coming, do come lovey do come. And then someone was bending down over her, saying, "It's a dear little boy."

Jean was ever so disappointed. She just shut her eyes and cried. To think it wasn't Daisy after all. It was through being away there in the hospital, and Norman so nasty over her, saying people was fed up. She didn't want to see Norman ever anymore. You stay with me, lovey, you stay like you used to.

She was ever so ill, and cried ever such a lot all the time, and everyone was ever so kind to her, only she was so disappointed it was a little boy and not a little girl, even, let alone Daisy; and she couldn't bear to have Norman come near her.

"You'd better go now," someone told him—Jean heard them. "She'll get over it by and by."

Daisy lovey don't go, stay with Jean, don't go lovey, don't go away from Jean, don't go away will you Daisy, don't go....

When she got better and they gave her the little boy it didn't seem as if it was hers. She didn't like it; she always did want a little girl. Whatever did you go and give me that for, Daisy duck? Or was it a little friend of yours you wanted put where you could find him? All right, I'll look after 'im for you, duckie; I'll bring him up fine just like what you want. Only I did want a little girl. If you and me could've been together it would've been ever so nice....

And then they had to take the little boy from her; she was making him wet, crying on him.

When she got a bit stronger and able to sit up, with him lying in his cot by her, she got used to him in a way. There was a lady in the next bed; she was waiting for her seventh. You must get ever so used to it by then, mustn't you?

"Didn't chew want a liddle boy, then?" the lady asked her once.

"No, I wanted a little girl, ever so."

"Ar, I know, dear liddle things. Priddy liddle things they c'n be. P'raps you'll 'ave one nex' time," the lady told her.

"Oo, there never won't be any next time!"

She wasn't going to have any more to do with Norman; she hated the sight of him, reely she did.

She used to sit there and cry, thinking how nasty he was over Daisy.

Once when he came he bent down and pointed to baby. "I had him called Leo," he told her. He gave her a wink. "Born under Leo."

She only stared at him.

"That do for you?"

"I don't care."

She used to turn her head away when he came to see her, and they stopped bringing him then.

She told the lady once, "I can't bear the sight of 'im."

"Ar, you'll ged over id. I was that way meself with me first. You'll ged over id alri'."

Then when it was time for her to go home they sent for him to fetch her back. "Your husband's downstairs waiting for you," they told her.

When she got down in the lift he was waiting for her with a taxi to take her and the baby home. The last time she'd been in a taxi with him was after the wedding.

She didn't take any notice of him. She couldn't think of anything but how tired she was, being up for so long, and how heavy baby was; she didn't know however to get him upstairs,

Norman had put a cot in the room, and she put baby in it, and had to see to him, and she could hardly drag herself about. She lay down on the outside of the bed.

Norman said, "I got some kippers for tea, will that do you?"

She nodded; she didn't care. Then she remembered, and got herself up again to cook them.

Norman was quite cheerful; he didn't seem to see she couldn't bear the sight of him. He got busy with his kipper, and then jerked his head over at the cot. "Good thing it was a boy, wasn't it?"

"I don't care."

He took a mouthful of tea. "Born under Leo, as I told you. Show you the chart in a minute. Good business."

She picked her kipper to pieces and spread it about on her plate.

When Norman had done he cleared a place with his arm and pulled the chart from his pocket and spread it out. "As I said, born under Leo. This should make him a leader of men; he will succeed in whatever he takes up. In the progressed chart a business career is clearly indicated. Perhaps a tendency to over-confidence which he will have to guard against. His best years will be the tenth, the nineteenth, the twenty-eighth—in these years it will pay him to throw his weight about..."

Everything was swimming round. She felt hot and cold, and sick with the scraps of kipper she had managed to swallow. Norman's voice was coming loud and soft and loud, in waves. When he came to the end of something and she didn't say anything he looked up: "Well? What about that."

"Norman," she managed to say, "I think I'll go to bed now."

"Just as you like." He folded the paper and put it back in his pocket, huffy with her. "I thought this would interest you, that's all."

When she got up the room swam round. She sat down again. "I keep coming over funny," she said.

Norman was all hurt and huffy; he was ramming his papers back in his attaché case. "Just as you like. Better turn in, then."

He jerked his head over at the cot. "Does he cry much?"

"I don't know. They used to take him away when he cried."

Norman cleared his throat; he got up and took his coat down from the door. "Well, I've been sleeping over at the studio when you weren't here. May as well, give you more room with the kid. Well, may as well go and turn in."

"All right," she said.

When he'd opened the door he turned round: "You can manage, can't you?"

"Yes. All right."

He shut the door. She went on sitting there until the baby woke up and began to cry and she had to get up and see to it.

She didn't care; she was glad Norman was out of the way.

He came back next day at tea-time and went out again later. Some time after, when it was a wet evening once, he said, "Not much point turning out again on a night like this. May as well stop."

"You'd better not," she told him. "Baby cries in the night, dreadful sometimes."

So he shrugged his shoulders and went out.

She didn't want Norman hanging round; she'd got used to him not being there. When she had to get up for baby she'd look round the empty room and think, Daisy duck, you're here, aren't you? The same you always were?

She used to go and stand by the cot and look at baby and think of Daisy looking at him too. Is he going to be psychic? Do tell me lovey, go on.

She'd think how Daisy must be whispering in his ear, telling him things. That's why you don't talk to me so much as you did, isn't it, duck?

It was lonely sometimes, though, with no one but baby there, and he couldn't say anything. He'd cry and wake her up, and she'd lie there wondering il she'd ever be able to go off in a trance again properly, and Daisy come, the way she did before. She hadn't done it since baby was born. Once she got up and went in the big room and put the lights on and sat down on one of the chairs with the big empty floor in front of her and waited to see if she'd go off. It took her ever so long, but she did hear Daisy at last, "Hallo, everybody!" so it was all right. You aren't stopping coming, Daisy duck, over baby, or him being nasty, are you, then?

One day when he was there he said, "Well, what about you getting going again? You've taken it easy about long enough, haven't you?"

"How d'you mean? The *séances*?"

"Exactly. Time we were getting something planned out. I was thinking of starting advertising next week if you're ready."

"I don't care," she said. "When you like. Daisy doesn't mind; she'll do it all right." She didn't look at him. She thought, It's more than you deserve from her, either.

"Now, look here," he said.

But she wouldn't look at him; she was turned away, seeing to baby. She heard him shove the plates away with his elbow.

"Look here, you've had all this time to think something up, and if you haven't done it you'd better get on with it now and do some thinking quick. What's wrong with something historical?

Ancient Egyptians. Or something from the Lost Continent might go well. Or if you can't do anything but children make it some kid from history. Little princes murdered in the Tower— wicked uncle. That'd go down. What's wrong with them?"

She turned round then and looked at him. "I don't know what you mean," she said. "Daisy brings who she likes; I can't help what she does. I'll ask her if you like. But sometimes she'll do it and sometimes she won't."

Norman slammed his fist on the table and half got up. You could see he was going to say something nasty, but then he didn't. If it was something about Daisy again he thought better of it. He shrugged his shoulders and reached round for his case with the papers in it. "Oh, all right, get on with it; have it your own way. Don't blame me when it's played out."

He ruled out a square on a sheet of paper and started writing in it. "When d'you want to start, then?"

"Any time. Daisy's ready; she doesn't mind."

"Sunday week, then." He set his face, huffy, and went on writing it out.

Sunday week the big room was full of people, fresh ones most of them. "Only one or two of the old lot," Norman whispered to her when he came to fetch her. She was in her long blue dress again, seeing to baby, so that he wouldn't cry while the people were there. She was ever so afraid he might. "What does he want to cry for?" Norman asked her. He was getting impatient, hurrying her up.

But when she got into the room she forgot all about baby; it was like old times, with them waiting for her, and her chair empty, up at the top, and the lights turned down. And she wasn't a bit afraid; she knew Daisy was waiting to come. Here I am, Jee-een, she kept saying, jumping up and down; Jean could see her ever so clear inside her head. All right, lovey, you wait a minute.

She sat down and shut her eyes. She heard Norman starting off beside her: "Ladies and gentlemen, there is no one present to-day who will not rejoice to hear that Madam Jan has returned from her travels and is here once more to bring you the little spirit-child Daisy." Then before he could say any more Daisy piped up loud, right against her ear, "Hallo, everybody, here I am!"

It was a good one, Norman said. A dozen or more got messages, and they were all ever so pleased, and they'd work up the connexion again in no time. "Perhaps you were right after all," he said, when he'd done showing them out. "Only the kid'll have to learn to keep his mouth shut."

He said you could hear him crying, quite plain, through the wall.

"Poor little mite, he isn't used to being left."

"He'd better get used, then."

Norman was pleased with the way it had gone, though, and so was Jean; it was a good job if it stopped Norman being nasty over Daisy. Thank you, Daisy love, she said, while she was tucking in baby. Thank you ever so much. And you will stop baby crying, won't you, lovey?

But then they started booking up private appointments again, and that was worse; it meant she had to leave baby any time. Sometimes she had two or three in a day. Norman stopped going to his studio except in the mornings, so that he could be there to let her clients in. He had to do his correspondence work in the room with baby while she was giving a sitting, and he got ever so cross when baby cried. "Why the hell can't you give it something to shut it up?"

"Poor little mite," she used to say, "he only wants to be picked up."

She was tired right out very soon, with appointments one after the other, and baby crying, and Norman at her all the time. If she hadn't been a lot stronger by now she couldn't have done it at all.

Baby got on Norman's nerves dreadful. "Put that brat down!" he shouted at her. "Holding him like that, messing up your dress." And yet he wouldn't let her see clients except in her velvet. And when she did put baby down he'd start cursing because of the noise he made. As soon as the last client had been he always packed up his books and cleared off for the night.

Jean was glad really, because then she hadn't got to bother. When baby cried she'd pick him up and rock him till he went to sleep. Daisy duck, she used to say sometimes when she was ever so tired, keep him quiet for me; can't you, lovey?

She put him back in the cot and tucked him in. "Be good boy then, Lee-o. Daisy'll look after you, won't you, lovey?"

Just sometimes she wished Norman would stay, when she was tired out, and be nice to her the way he used to. One afternoon she had three ladies on end, and it was six o'clock before she'd done. Her nerves were all on edge, and she thought she'd scream if baby didn't quiet down; she'd heard him on and off through the wall.

But when she got in the back-room baby was asleep, for a wonder—cried himself to sleep. Norman was sitting at the table doing his work in his shirt-sleeves; he started to pack his papers away when he saw her come in.

"That the last?"

"That's all," she said. She sat down suddenly, tired right out. Then she remembered not to crush her frock, and got up again to take it off.

She hung it up behind the curtain on the wall, and when she turned round he was putting on his coat, getting ready to go. "Norman," she said all at once, faint-feeling.

"Well?" He was straightening his tie.

She went over slowly, and stood by his elbow. "Norman?"

"Well, what?"

He looked round, impatient of her.

"Don't go," she said.

His face changed all at once; he looked like he used to back at Madam Eva's. She could feel her heart beating in her ears.

"So that's it," he said, with a slow smile, like he used to have. He stood and looked at her for a minute.

And then he took hold of her, ever so rough, not like he used to. But Jean didn't care; she started to cry, she was so happy.

When he went out next day she told Daisy, You don't mind, do you, Daisy duck? I can't help being fond of him, reely I can't. And he won't go saying any more about you, I know he won't. You don't mind, do you?

After that Norman arranged with the lady downstairs to take baby in the afternoons. He was getting quite big now, starting to crawl about, and Norman said he couldn't be bothered with having him round while Jean was seeing clients. Norman only went out in the mornings now, while Jean tidied up the place and put the big room ready for the afternoon and took baby out while she did the shopping. Then at dinner-time she cleaned him up and took him downstairs—"Now be good boy, Lee-o"—and left him there before she got changed ready for people coming.

He wasn't so much bother at night either now he was bigger; and Norman got some stuff from the chemist he said he'd give him if he did wake up, to make him go off again. "It looks as if we'd got over that all right," he said.

He was nice to her now, like he was before baby came. When Jean was tired out after appointments he'd make her come over and sit on his knee like he used to, and she'd go all limp against his shoulder and have a good cry. Oh, he was lovely to her now!

Sometimes she'd remember: "It's ever so late: I ought to go and fetch up Lee-o, oughtn't I?"

But he'd say, "Let him alone; he's all right."

They were making such a lot of money now he didn't mind paying the lady downstairs an hour or two extra for looking after Leo.

Ever so many were coming to the *séances* now. Norman got in a lot more chairs, and they stood two deep all round the room. When they were pulled out for the *séance* the people were sitting one behind the other like in a theatre. Norman said they'd get a larger flat later on, where she could have a little room special for private sittings— "more intimate," was what he said; "they like that," as well as the big room. Then he wouldn't have to put the chairs back three times a week as he did now; they were having the *séance* now three times a week. "Sure you're not getting tired," he asked her. "Not getting stale, are you?"

But she wasn't; she liked it. She liked the feeling Daisy was happy now, helping people. "So long as she's happy, so'm I."

Norman didn't say anything against Daisy either now, now it was all going on well. "I told you he'd be all right, didn't I, lovey?"

Norman said, too, that in a bit when they got a larger flat there'd be room for Leo to play about without getting in people's way, and he wouldn't have to he put downstairs anymore.

Jean did wonder if he was going to be psychic. She used to watch him in the mornings when he was playing round and she was doing her work. Daisy duck, do say something to him and see if he'll hear you, do. But he never seemed to take any notice.

Once she picked him up and held him and asked him if he didn't hear any little girl talking to him. But he only stared at her and wriggled to be put down.

She said it to Norman once: "Do you think he'll be psychic, Norman? He never seems to hear Daisy, though I can swear she's there talking to him. Will he only get it when he grows up? It seems so funny doesn't it, with both of us?"

Norman gave her a sharp look. "That's an idea," he said. "All right, you get on and train him up young. No harm, even if he takes to something else later. You ought to have him with you more," he said. "We'll see about it later on."

"I have asked Daisy," she said, "if he's psychic, but she won't tell me."

She used to watch him playing in the mornings by himself.

"Don't you see a little girl, Lee-o, that's playing with you? Ever such a pretty little girl with curly hair and blue eyes."

He stared at her.

"Don't you ever see her, Lee-o?"

"No," he said. He was talking now, nearly two. "Don't you ever see pictures and things, Lee-o? You tell Mum. Don't you ever see pretty pictures when you go to sleep?"

"No. Don't."

Norman asked, one dinner-time, "Is he any good?"

"I don't think he's psychic a bit, Norman. It's ever so funny."

"Pity, that. Child medium. Would have gone like hot cakes. Never mind, may do better at something else. It's a risky business."

He didn't take much notice of Leo except to tell him to be quiet, he didn't seem to care about him not hearing Daisy. But Jean was ever so upset about it. She used to ask Daisy, Do make him psychic, there's a dear. Why ever don't you? You do want him to talk to, don't you, as well as me?

She thought sometimes how if he could do it too when he got bigger she wouldn't have to do so much. She was getting tired a bit, with everyone wanting to talk to Daisy. Three *séances* a week and private sittings two or three a day, on and on, it was enough to tire anyone out. Norman was ever so pleased, though. He got himself a new velvet coat and Jean a new dress for sittings, and he said next year when they'd got a nice bit behind them they'd move into the bigger flat. He didn't notice when Jean was faintish once or twice. But then she found she was going to have another baby.

When she first knew it it was one morning while Norman was out. And she didn't know what to do; she felt so dreadful thinking what Norman would say. Oh Daisy, do take it away, do. You know I can't ever let Norman know, you know how it was last time. You know I can't, reely I can't.

Leo was playing with his soldiers; he scrambled up and toddled over to her. "Mum," he said. "Soldjer broke."

"All right, lovey," she said, not listening to him. "Mum'll see to it."

He went off again, and she went on sitting there. I never can, you know I can't. Do help me lovey, do help me out of it.

But she couldn't even hear Daisy speak to her.

She went on for days not daring to tell him. Do help me, lovey, she'd say, stirring the soup. You know I'm not any good to you when I'm like that, don't you now. Go on Daisy do, do help me.

In the afternoon she'd put on her new blue frock and see clients; and there was Norman, in between, sitting there doing his work at the table, in his shirt-sleeves with his new velvet coat hung over a chair; and she didn't know what to do, thinking how she'd have to tell him.

It preyed on her mind so she could hardly get off in sittings, thinking, How is it Daisy can help out everyone else and she can't tell me anything. Oh do lovey, do take it away, don't let it happen.

And once in a *séance* she took so long to go off she could hear Norman's voice going on and on. He'd got as far as saying, "This little spirit-child who is with us here to-day, ready and eager to help you all speak with your dear ones…" And she still hadn't got off. He had to go on saying some more. "This little girl left the earth more than twenty years ago. She is with us still; she is as young as ever she was." He stopped, and then he had to go on again. "Young in heart and soul. She knows all your troubles, and she's going to bring your dear ones to help you in them. The one thing she is anxious to do is help us who remain on this sorrowful earth, full of sorrow and trouble…"

It was only then that she heard his voice go faint, and Daisy come and say, "Hallo, everybody!"

"What on earth was the matter with you?" he asked her afterwards.

"I don't know, Norman. Daisy wouldn't come. She's tired, I expect."

And he gave her a sharp look; it made her heart turn over. "Ease off for a day or two if you like?"

But she shook her head. "No, it's all right."

Then the next week at a *séance* she fainted instead of going off.

When she came round she was lying down in the back room, and Norman was ever so cross.

"What's the idea?" he said. "What's the matter with you? My having to send everyone away," he said, "and see to you at the same time. Why couldn't you say before if you felt ill?"

Jean felt dreadful; she just said, "I'm going to have another baby."

Norman was in such a rage he went red and then white and he could hardly speak. "You fool!" he said.

He came over close, and she thought for a minute he was going for her. He was dead-white and shaking all over. "How could you be such a fool?" he said.

She shut her eyes and began to cry, and she heard him go out after a minute and slam the door.

He came back middle-day the next day. Leo was playing on the floor, and Norman swore at him and told him to clear off downstairs out of the way.

"He can't go down by himself, poor little mite."

Norman wouldn't look at her. She took Leo downstairs, and when she came back he only said, You've got an appointment at two. You can do that, I suppose."

She nodded. She got into her frock.

He sat there through the afternoon, doing his work, letting people in. "This way, my dear lady," she could hear him say, out on the stairs. When the last client had gone he looked at her for the first time. "Anyone would think you did it on purpose, to put the lid on it every time we're getting on."

He was putting on his coat. "I suppose you've forgotten last time," he said—"the time it took you getting right afterwards. If you were like anyone else," he said, getting sorry for himself, "you wouldn't waste so much time over it, anyhow. And you know that, and yet there you go again...."

He threw his books in his case.

"Oh, Norman, you aren't going, are you?"

"Yes, I am," he said. "I'm fed up with you—fed up. You just do it out of spite."

He went out, and she sat down and cried.

After that he only came in for appointments, and he wouldn't take any notice of her. He sat at the table doing his own work, and when the clients had gone he went too; he didn't take any notice when she tried to speak to him.

She fetched Leo up and put him to bed, and then she sat there keeping quiet not to wake him, and talked to Daisy. Daisy love, do help me out, why ever don't you, why ever did you let this happen. It isn't you this time, is it Daisy duck?

She started being sick at night, and when she had to get up it woke Leo and he cried. She didn't know what to do. One morning she dressed him and took a Tube and took him home to Mum and asked her to keep him till it was over.

Mum and Dad were ever so upset to see her look so bad, and they wanted her to stop there, only she had to get back for the *séance* at five.

Norman didn't notice for several days that Leo wasn't there. Then he said, "Where's the kid?"

"I took him home to Mum."

He grunted.

Jean was all alone then, except when there were clients there. There was no one to talk to, but Daisy. Daisy was ever so sweet. Here I am, Jee-een! she'd say, when Jean had been up in the night and was lying awake, chilled right through, not knowing what to do. Or when Jean was sweeping out the big room, ready for the afternoon: Jee-een! You'll be all right! Oh Daisy, I do wish I would.

She went home once to see Leo. She told Mum, "I don't know what I'd do if it wasn't for Daisy."

Norman asked her—it was one of the few times he spoke to her—"I suppose you'll have to go to the hospital again?"

"I don't know," she told him. "Daisy says I'll be all right."

He was brushing down his coat, ready to go. "You and your Daisy," he said. "I've heard enough of your blasted Daisy, understand?"

He threw down the brush.

"Oh Norman, your own little sister!"

"Sister," he said, picking up his hat. "I never had any sister, thank God."

He saw her then; she was almost in a faint, leaning back, holding on to the table. He smiled slowly. "D'you hear?" he said. "I never had any sister Daisy."

He put on his hat and went out.

F

"Now what I say is, you're sceptic. Yes, you are; I can see you are. Now you can't do anything for someone is sceptic. If you believed in it I could tell you something would 'elp you out. An' what I tell you is, you re meetin' your troubles 'alf-way. Now what you gotter do is believe in what I'm tellin' you. Nothing ever come of bein' sceptic. Now does it? Now I'm askin' you. 'Ave you 'ad a lotter luck in your life? No. Well, there you are. Now if you wasn't sceptic you'd see the truth of what I'm sayin'. Nothin' ever come of bein' sceptic, so you listen to what I'm tellin' you. An' what I'm tellin' you is, you're meetin' your troubles 'alf-way. So now you just stop bein' sceptic—it never did anyone any good—an' listen to what I got to tell you."

VII

Jean was very, very ill—much more ill than she was with Leo. There was Daisy, and Norman saying no Daisy. Don't go, Daisy duck, don't take any notice of 'im what he says, don't, don't let 'im come, don't Daisy duck, don't....

The sister was the same one; she came along saying, "Well, you've got your little girl this time Mrs. Mitch, aren't you pleased?"

It isn't you is it, Daisy duck, you're there, aren't you, like you always were. Don't take any notice of him, don't let him come, don't Daisy.

When she came out it was Madam Eva who fetched her. She said Jean was coming home with her for a bit. She put Jean in a taxi, and Jean sat back in the corner holding baby, until Madam Eva said she'd take her, and then she just sat holding nothing and watching the streets go by.

Madam Eva was ever so talkative. She wanted to get Jean talking. "It'll be a nice little change for you, being 'ome with us for a bit. Make a bit of a break for you, won't it? Not having any 'ouse-work for a bit, only baby to look after. She's a sweet little thing, isn't she? Mr. Harsett's ever so curious to see 'er, he's always a one for babies; you ought to've seen 'im with my Elsie. He'll be spoiling 'er till there's no holding 'er, won't 'e, woopsie-poopsie?"

Jean watched the streets go by—they all looked like one another—and the rain was pouring down. A winter baby, going home in the rain. Madam Eva kept rattling on, wanting to get Jean talking. "Well," she said, "you've never asked where Norman's got to."

She was fussing with baby, pulling the shawl round her. She gave Jean a sideways look, but Jean didn't take any notice. "You'll be seeing 'im before very long, I expect; 'e'll be along looking for you. I expect he's downright sorry 'e couldn't come along to-day."

She looked round sharp then, but Jean didn't turn her head. "There, woopsie, diddums, wasn't it cumfy then? 'E's away on business just now."

Jean looked round slowly, and then she took it in. "All right, I'm going home, then." She turned back and watched the streets going by.

Madam Eva gave a jump; she went rattling on. "You're coming 'ome with me duckie for a bit. He'll be back presently, I expect, wanting you 'ome. You'll be able to go 'ome then with the little baby and 'ave the little boy back too. When she's got a bit bigger she won't be such a handful, will she woodlums, then? I'll be able to give you a hand with 'er for the first few days while you're finding your feet."

Jean sat up straight. "I'm going home."

Madam Eva didn't know what to do. "No, you aren't. Not just for a bit. Come along now," she coaxed her. "Come on, love. You come with me for a bit; it'll be a lot better for you, starting off with; it'll do you a lot more good."

Jean sat bolt upright, staring ahead; she was in a sweat from weakness. "I'm going home now. Tell 'im—tell the man. I'm going home along with Daisy."

Madam Eva gave a great sigh; she didn't know what to do. In the end she put her head out of the window and told the man to turn back the other way.

"I don't know, I'm sure; I don't know what you're goin' to do."

When the taxi'd turned round Jean lay back and shut her eyes.

Madam Eva was sighing and puffing. "I don't know; I don't know what to say. You can't stay there by yourself. I don't know what Mr. Harsett will say when I get back and tell 'im; he said to be sure to bring you. I don't know what to do with you, I reely don't."

Jean opened her eyes and looked at her. "What did he say that for, about Daisy not being his sister?"

Madam Eva gave a jump and a sigh; she started twitching again at baby's shawl. "What? 'Oo did? Norman Mitch? Did 'e say that? He must've been cracked. I wonder whatever 'e said that for."

"He said he never had any sister Daisy."

"Did 'e, now? Well, what a thing to say. Did 'e have any sister? Well, now, you're asking me. 'Ow do I know? I 'aven't known Norman Mitch all 'is life. He ought to know, didn't 'e? I expect he was only having 'is joke."

Jean shut her eyes again; she didn't say anything.

Madam Eva fidgeted about; she couldn't leave it alone. "I'll tell you what I'd do if I were you; I'd ask Daisy 'erself. You ask 'er some time if she's 'is sister or if she isn't; she ought to know, didn't she?"

Jean didn't say anything; she lay back and let the taxi rock her till it stopped.

Madam Eva carried baby upstairs. When they got there it looked as if Norman had been living there some time; the place was all upside down, and there was a dirty frying-pan on the stove. But it had been shut up for days; you could tell that, it was so stuffy.

Madam Eva sat Jean down on a chair and puffed around, getting a kettle to boil. "You won't hardly have room here, will you, now, with the two of them? Cramped up all together. Keeping you in a little pig-hole of a place like this. I always told him. One room, isn't it, that's all it comes to, with the front kept for clients. I expect you won't be starting again for a bit, will you? I'd use that room if I was you."

Jean let her rattle on; she wasn't listening. She sat with baby on her lap, until Madam Eva took her from her and put her in the cot. "Poor little mite! What did you call 'er?"

"Janet. After Mum."

"Ar, dear little thing."

Madam Eva went down to the shops and fetched up some ham for tea and made Jean eat it. "You can't stay here alone with the little baby, though, can you?"

"I did before."

Madam Eva didn't say anything to that. "Have you got any money?"

"Money? No. I don't know."

Madam Eva said "tut-tut" and "tsh-tsh." "Well, here you are— 'ere's some. I'll get it from 'im."

"I don't like leaving you, I reely don't. I don't like thinking of it. Change your mind and come 'ome? Come on."

Jean shook her head. "I'd rather be here; I've got things to do."

"Well, you know your own business, I expect. Mind you let me know, now, if you want anything."

When she'd gone Jean sat on and on and it began to get dark. She wished in a way she'd gone with Madam Eva, in case Norman should come in. He won't, though. He won't, will he, lovey? You and me have got it to ourselves; we've got to get this straight. You're here all right, aren't you, duck? It feels ever so empty. Won't you say something to me?

She sat on and on till it was dark, waiting for Daisy to come and talk to her. Baby was quiet; she was ever so good—not like Leo used to be.

When it was dark she got up and put the light on and drew the blind. She was stiff and cold, but she didn't feel tired anymore; she was doing things in a dream; she had to find out for sure about Daisy. P'raps she'd tell me better in her own room.

The front room hadn't been opened up for weeks; it smelt stuffy and shut-up, like a tomb. The curtains were left drawn back, and you could see the houses across the street shining a bit where it was raining. The chairs were stood tidy round the walls, and it was all thick with dust. She tried to draw the curtains, but they were too heavy for her; she put all the lights on and sat down near the door, facing the black windows, and clenched her hands together. Daisy, come and tell me, do come.

She could feel the sweat coming out on her while she sat all clenched and tense. It was like years ago when she first tried to learn to concentrate, back at Madam Eva's. Daisy, if you aren't his sister then who are you?

There wasn't anything; the room was big and empty. Daisy'd gone, Daisy wouldn't come anymore, Daisy you must come, you must tell me, go on, go on do—just this once, Daisy.

She couldn't go on concentrating; she was tired out. She sagged back and cried a bit with tiredness. Oh Daisy duck, do tell me. I must know—are you reely there? Are you reely someone else, or is it true what he said, aren't you there at all? That's what he meant, didn't he? He was only being nasty wasn't he? Go on, do say.

She held her breath to hear Daisy say it, Hallo, Jee-een! the way she always did, in her head. But she never did, it was only Jean wishing it, it wasn't any good. It's because I'm so tired, isn't it, Daisy duck, you can't come? You'll come another day, won't you, lovey, when I can get off properly, and you can come and talk to people the way you like? You will, won't you, love?

She got up, so tired she didn't know what to do, and put the lights out and shut up the big room. Baby was awake now, wanting her bottle. Jean gave it to her; she was a funny little thing, darkhaired. She never could be you, could she, duck? That isn't why you don't come, is it?

But she was too tired out to care, almost.

Next day she dusted out the front room. Daisy wasn't there; you could tell that. Jean felt dull, as if it didn't matter. She isn't anywhere; I know that all right. That's what he meant, there never was any Daisy, he made it up. It isn't any good. What's the good trying.

She dusted all the chairs and stood them back straight as they were before, with their backs to the wall.

Only when she got back in the other room she couldn't believe it—that there wasn't any Daisy. She couldn't believe it, that's all. It isn't true, is it, lovey, you're there all right. It's only that you don't want to come and talk just now. You like me to talk to you, don't you, duck. You'd feel lonely if I didn't take any notice.

When she'd had dinner she sat on at the table, sipping a cup of tea. Baby was lying quite good in her cot; she was a dear little thing, ever so good. It might be her, after all. How could it be, though, if there never was any Daisy. Yes, but if it wasn't his little sister it was someone else; what's it matter? Maybe her name isn't Daisy at all, but something else. But you don't mind what I call you, do you, duck? You and me know each other by this time.

Madam Eva came next day to see how she was getting on. "Sure you can manage on your own?"

Madam Eva wasn't cheery like her usual self, but all fussed up and worried and in a hurry to get away, even though she didn't like going and leaving Jean.

Jean asked her, "You know Daisy..."

"I wouldn't go fretting myself," Madam Eva told her, "if I was you. I wouldn't think of trying to take a client for a week or two; I reely wouldn't. What you want's a good rest. I wouldn't go worrying my 'ead over it."

But Jean wasn't going to be put off. "If it isn't Daisy, who is it then? Who is it does the talking?"

Madam Eva sat back and fanned herself with her glove. "Oh, dear, I don't know! I wouldn't worry my 'ead." And then she leaned over and poured herself another cup. "It's some other little girl, I expect. That's who it would be. You can depend upon it. Some little girl that wants to come back and talk, anyhow, isn't she?"

Jean didn't know what to think. Sometimes she'd think, That's right; what does it matter? If it isn't her it's someone else. You're the same, aren't you, lovey, whatever anyone calls you? Other times when she was doing out the big room, thinking of when they used to have the *séances* there, she'd think, It isn't that, though. If Norman made it up about Daisy it isn't true, any of it. There aren't any spirits. Then who is it talks to people, then—all those that Daisy used to bring? People used to talk to them; they knew who it was all right. He can't have made that up.

When she was back doing the washing up, giving baby her bottle, she'd say, Daisy duck, you don't mind me doubting about you, do you? You know I've got to get it straight; I can't go deceiving people if that's what he wants. He isn't coming anymore, though, is he? I don't think he is, do you?

She went home to see Mum when she got a bit stronger, and took baby to show her. Mum and Dad were shocked to hear about Norman not coming home all that time. Mum gave her some money, and said she'd send Auntie Lil to find out from Madam Eva where he'd gone and make him come home.

"I don't want him," Jean said.

Leo was grown ever such a big boy. Mum said to leave him there. "You can't do with two, on your own like that."

Dad asked if she was working now, and she said no.

When Dad had gone out she asked Mum, "You know my Daisy. You know the spirits that talk...."

"You know I don't hold with it," Mum said. "I never did."

"Only what is it, Mum? Is it real? Don't you know what it is? You always said Granny could do it."

"It's the Sight," Mum told her. "It's yourself. You know things other people don't, and see things they don't—that's all."

"But, Mum, all these people who come, I don't know them. I'm gone right off in a trance. I don't know who they want to talk to. It must be something, Mum, reely it must."

"Some can do it and some can't," was all Mum would say. "And no good ever came of it."

It isn't me, though, is it, duck, it's you, only I don't know who you are. Why don't you come and talk to me anymore? Do come, there's a dear.

Norman came home soon after that. He came in one day when Jean was busy, washing out baby's things, up to her elbows in soapsuds in the sink. She heard him come in, but she didn't turn round or say anything.

She heard him fidgeting about, and presently he said, "If that's all the welcome I get I'll go again."

She turned round and looked at him.

He was standing by the cot, watching baby. He'd got fatter, bloated-looking.

"So that's the kid," he said.

He was awkward; he didn't know what to say. He came over to the window and stood looking out, tapping his feet on the floor. Jean went on with her washing.

"Where's the boy?"

"Home with Mum."

He turned round presently. "Well, are you ready to start work again?"

"No."

"You don't mind taking your time, do you?"

She went on rinsing and wringing out.

He began to whistle and went back to the table; she heard him put some money on it. "Here, that's for you and the kids."

When he opened the door she turned round: "I didn't know what you wanted baby called."

"Call it any damn' thing you like."

He'd gone again.

He came back on and off and gave her money to go on with. He didn't take any notice of her except to ask her if she meant to start work again. Sometimes she said no, and sometimes she didn't answer. Whichever she did he only sneered at her. Then he'd go and snap his fingers at baby Janet to make her look at him, but it only frightened her and made her cry. He didn't stay more than a few minutes.

Jean fetched Leo back later on when she got stronger, and when Norman found him there, playing with the toy train his grandad gave him, he started talking to him, pretending to play too. It was only to make Jean take notice of him. She'd be sewing or washing or heating up baby's bottle, and not say anything.

He was funny and awkward with the children, and they didn't like him. You could see he only took notice of them to make Jean say something, or because he thought she wouldn't like it. Baby was frightened of him and cried when he came near. Then Jean picked her up and rocked her till she was quiet. He'd look at her to see if she'd tell him off; then he'd have been nasty. But she didn't.

He tried to make friends with Leo. "Well, my young man," he'd say, bending down over his stomach, with his thumbs tucked in his armholes, "and how does the train run to-day?" With his voice soft, the way he knew how to make it.

But Leo only stared up at him, quite solemn.

And when he bent right down to join in the game his hand would shake and he'd push the engine off the rails or knock over a signal, and Leo would crawl over and solemnly put it back.

"Well, my young man," Norman asked him once, "and what are you going to be when you grow up? Going to call spirits from the vasty deep, like Mum?"

He took a sideways look at Jean, but she wouldn't look up.

He drew in his breath between his teeth: "Or going to be a professor, like Dad?"

"Going to be engine-driver."

Norman gave a laugh at that and patted him on the head and made him look up by giving him a penny. "See here, Sonny, when you've got enough pennies you can get a new engine."

But he wasn't thinking about the child; you could see that. He was wondering about Jean; how much she minded what he'd said about her. But she wasn't going to show him.

He was going on at Leo: "What do you say when someone gives you something?"

He turned round sharp on Jean—the first time he had spoken to her that day. "Can't you teach him his manners?"

Say thank you, Lee-o," she told him, without looking up.

The child mumbled it. He went on staring at Norman to see what he'd do next. But Norman shrugged his shoulders and turned away; he was tired of him.

When he'd shut the door behind him Jean asked Daisy, Don't let him come anymore, lovey. Make him go off and leave us in peace. We don't want him here, do we, duck.

Leo was playing with his train and his penny, putting it in the truck and wheeling it on and taking it out again. He was busy talking to himself all the time, but he wasn't old enough to talk to her. And Janet didn't do anything but make little noises all on her own. It was as good as being alone. She couldn't help talking to Daisy sometimes, just for company. Lee-o's getting a big boy, isn't he, lovey? You'll help me to bring him up nice, won't you? I don't want him taking after Norman.

But she didn't try to go right off anymore. Daisy didn't want to tell her who she was, and she wouldn't do it without knowing. You'll let me know soon enough when you want to talk, won't you, duck? If you ever do. I shall know all right when you're wanting it.

She was kept busy, with the children to look after. They had to be taken out some time. She did up her work in the mornings and took them down with her in the afternoon to do the shopping.

Leo could walk by himself now if they didn't go too far; but Janet was getting a big girl too, and ever so heavy to carry. Jean thought sometimes she ought to have a pram, or get Mum to let her have the old mailcart for Janet when she got a bit bigger, only she never would be able to get it upstairs.

She didn't go very far, only to the two or three shops. Leo only toddled along, catching on to her, and she had to hold up Janet and her parcels at the same time. She was glad to get in a shop and rest her arm on the counter while she waited.

Once there was a little girl, ever so sweet. It might have been the very same one she saw that time when Leo was on the way. The very spit of Daisy. Well, you didn't mean to come to me, did you, lovey?

She sighed and stood up straight again, taking Janet's weight from where she'd been resting her on the counter. She put the basket down in her other hand and told Leo to hold on to it. She was terrified he'd let go, out in the street. She only went to one more shop, and then they climbed the stairs again, back at home.

Janet had to have her bottle and be put to sleep, and then Jean gave Leo his tea and had her own. Afterwards, when she'd cleared up, she'd have to mend his jersey he'd got on and swill it out.

One evening when she'd got them both to bed and was sitting there mending Norman came in. She knew who it was before he opened the door. He didn't often come so late. She didn't look up; she thought he'd go over and talk to Leo like he always did, lucky Leo hadn't gone off to sleep yet.

Norman came in and sat at the table and threw his hat on it. She bent down a bit lower, looking at her stitches.

"So that's all you've got to say to me."

She looked up. "Leo's awake, if you want to see him."

Norman pushed his hat further away and pulled his attaché case up on the table. "What I've come for," he said, snapping open the catches, one and then the other, "is to talk business."

He slapped out a pad and unclipped his pen from his pocket and opened it.

"Do you happen to realize," he said, "you've been eating your head off here for the last six months?"

Jean bit off a piece of cotton. "What do you want me to do? I've got to look after the children. We've got to eat."

"I'm glad you realize it," he said, with his usual sort of sneer. "When d'you mean to start, then?"

He was drawing out a square on his pad, writing inside: "MAD-AME JEANNE, the world-famous..."

"Well—when?"

He went on writing, "trance medium," and then he stopped and looked up.

"Come on, when d'you want to start? Sunday? Sunday week?"

She wouldn't look at him, and he began getting sorry for himself. "You can't say I don't give you enough time. I'd like to know who'd give you six months off and say nothing. Keeping you here eating your head off with the two kids, after all I've spent getting you launched.... I'm not made of money."

She looked up then at him, and he looked down quickly and went on writing. "...has returned and will open a new series..."

"All right," she said, "I'll go out to work." She jerked her head at the paper; "I'm not going to do that anymore."

Norman went pink and then white and threw down his pen. "What the hell!" he said. "What's the idea? Have you gone clean off your head?"

The pen rolled along the table and fell to the floor; Norman got down off his chair to look for it.

Jean put down her sewing. While he was out of sight she leaned on the table and stared across at his chair and the writing-pad with the big letters at the top: "MADAME JEANNE..."

"I'm not going to do it," she said, "because it's all lies."

Norman came up from under the table. He was red from

stooping, and he looked at her as if he'd like to kill her. She flinched when she met his eyes, and then she went on looking at him.

Leo was calling out, back in the bed, "Dad, Dad!"

"What the devil do you mean, lies? What the devil's the matter with you?"

She looked at him, straight, and he started writing again, chewing his lips.

"Dad, Dad!"

"Shut your blasted mouth!"

"It's lies," she said. "You told me it was. I didn't know, or I wouldn't have done it. You told me it was all lies about Daisy— how you never had any sister."

"Sister be damned!"

He was dead-white now. His hand was shaking while he went on writing, "commencing Sunday the..."

"Your blasted Daisy!" he said. "I told you months ago that was played out. You wouldn't listen; you thought you knew everything— better than anyone else. I'm not going to have any more of it," he said. "The public's sick of it, and so am I. You'll find a new guide—and find one quick, or I'll find it for you."

When he stopped talking there was a bead of foam at the corner of his mouth.

"If Daisy's lies," she said dully, "then it's all lies. There aren't any spirits. It's lies; I'm not going to do it."

"You blasted fool!" He wiped his mouth with the back of his hand. "What's that got to do with it. It's your business, isn't it? What you're brought up to—and what I've trained you for? D'you think I'm going to waste all the time and money I've spent getting you started? What about my reputation? Fat lot you think about that! Your own blasted whimseys are all you can think about."

"I can't help it," she said. "If it isn't true I can't do it."

"True!" he said. "True, you..." He wiped his mouth again. "Do it? Of course you can do it. If you can't do it, what can you do?"

"I can work. I've worked before now—honest work."

"Honest! Honest be... Work?" he said. "Fat lot of work you can do, with a parcel of kids to look after."

"All right," she said, "I'll starve then. I'll go home. I don't care what I do." She wasn't looking at him now; she was looking down at the table, at Leo's knickers with the patch half sewn in. She was near crying. "All right, if you don't want to keep us me and the children will go home. I don't care; Dad'll keep them. And I can work then."

"Don't be a bloody fool!" he said.

When he saw her beginning to cry he puffed himself up; he knew he'd get the better of her now.

"You're talking like a fool," he said. "Just because this Daisy stunt's fallen through.... And I told you it would—you can't say I didn't. As if you could throw up the whole thing like that, with the connexion you've got, and the hold on the public.... You could start anything fresh you liked, within reason, and put it over."

"If Daisy's lies," she said, "it's all lies." She put her head down on the table and cried.

Look here," he said, "some people would lose their tempers with you. But I happen to know you've got these powers, and I'm ready to make allowances for a certain amount...a certain amount, mind," he said, "of temperament. That's to be expected. Now I'm ready to give you time, lake another week—a fortnight. Take three weeks if you like! So long as you come out with something constructive at the end of it."

She sobbed.

"Look here," he said. "Come to that I don't see why you shouldn't go on with the Daisy stunt if you're set on it. The public's had six months to forget it in. It'll go over for a bit longer. Then you can start something fresh next season."

Jean looked up. "Daisy's lies. You said so."

"Almighty God!" he said. "First you say one thing and then

another. You want this Daisy and then you don't want her. What the devil do you want?"

Jean wiped her eyes. "Daisy's lies—then it's all lies. There aren't any spirits. Then what is it that talks?"

"What! How the devil do I know? You ought to know—you've done it long enough."

Jean put her head down and cried again. "It's lies; I can't do it."

Norman slammed his pad on the table. "I've had enough of this! Do you hear?"

Leo woke up and started to cry: "Mum, Mum!"

"I tell you I've had enough! Temperament's one thing.... You'll start Sunday week, whether you like it or not. You'll make it Daisy or something else, you can please yourself—but you'll start! "

He threw his pad in his case and snapped the catch to and put on his hat. "See? You'll start Sunday week. I shall be in before that."

He went away, leaving her crying at the table and Leo crying over in the bed. She sat with her head on her arms. I can't Daisy duck, I can't. If it isn't true I can't do it, you know I can't, don't you, love. You don't mind do you, you know I can't do it if it isn't true.

Then she heard Leo calling out, and wiped her eyes and went over to him. "What is it, Leo?"

"Nasty man."

"That's all right," she told him. "It's only Dad." She hugged him up to her. "There, go to sleep, Lee-o."

You know, don't you duck, you know I can't.

I can't do it if it isn't true, can I? You know I can't, don't you duck.

Next day, after dinner, she dressed the children and took them on the bus and went to see Madam Eva. She hadn't been back there since the wedding. It was funny looking down over, seeing the blue bowl with yellow flowers in it stuck in the window, the same as ever. She opened the gate and it made the same noise it always did. It might have been one of the days she'd just run out to shop. Then she jumped up Janet on her right arm and turned round and put her left round Leo to lift him down the steps. By the time they were down she couldn't see over the curtain if there was a client there; she ought to have noticed from the top.

When she rang she heard Madam Eva come out of the front room. "Oo, I never ought to have rung, bringing you out!"

Madam Eva looked quite her old self, seeing her again with her hat off and her hair done tidy all over like a grey cap, like it always was, and smiling like old times. She gave Jean a poke, and sent her through to wait in the kitchen till she'd done.

It wasn't time for Mr. Harsett to be back, and the kitchen was empty, with the fire banked up. Jean sat Leo in Madam Eva's big basket-chair, where he couldn't get in any mischief. The kitchen was just the same as ever: the table scrubbed, and the same crockery hanging up, and the pile of books with the torn old "Ephemeris" on top behind the plates on the dresser. And outside the window there was the yard with the coal-house door ajar, and the tin roof from next door sticking up over the wall. Only it all wasn't quite real. It was Jean who was wrong.

She walked up and down with Janet to keep her quiet, and then she heard Madam Eva letting out her client and her coming tapping back with her little steps along the passage.

"There now, that's the last for to-day, unless there's any unexpected. There now, wopsie-popsie, come to Auntie Eva. There, isn't she a big girl?"

Jean stretched herself when Madam Eva took Janet from her. She said, "We never ought to have come this time of day when you're busy. I didn't think."

"Don't you fret yourself; it's good to see you." Madam Eva'd got Janet up in her arm; she put the kettle on with her other hand. And then she turned round and looked sharp at Jean: "Well, then? What's up?"

Jean didn't say at first. "I only want to talk to you."

"Go on, then." Madam Eva pulled out a chair and sat down with Janet on her knee. "Has 'e come back?"

"On and off. He came yesterday."

"Ar."

Leo was jumping up and down in the basket-chair: "Mum, Mum."

"Keep quiet, Lee-o."

"You keep still, lovey, and Auntie Eva'll give you something nice." She reached round and gave him a biscuit off the dresser. "Well?"

"He wants me to start next week."

"Does 'e, then? Well, we've all got to work, haven't we? There, lovey duck, you go to sleepy-byes."

Jean said, "When it started—you know, about Daisy: about me going off—was it always Daisy?"

"Eh? When you were back 'ere doing it?"

"Yes. Those first times. Was it Daisy then?"

Madam Eva thought a minute. "Not at the very start it wasn't."

"Who was it, then?"

"I don't know, my duck."

Jean was drawing patterns on the table. "Daisy's lies. He made it up, Norman did. All he says is lies."

"Oh, come now, come! Anyone can make a mistake, can't they? There, my wopsie-popsie!"

"What I want to know is—was there anything before? What was it that happened those first times when I used to go off?"

Madam Eva jogged Janet up and down. "I couldn't remember rightly. It was all about 'ow lovely it was over on the other side. You'd say, 'It's lovely over 'ere; it's all flowers and little birdies, ever so sweet'—and things of that sort. And if someone asked you a question you'd answer, most times."

"And then he said it was Daisy?"

"He said 'e thought it might've been."

"But it was only me saying it."

"It wasn't you, duck—you was gone off. It was the spirits talkin' through you."

Jean got up; she couldn't keep still. She turned round and looked out of the window. "How can you tell what it is?—that's what bothers me. How do you know it's spirits? It might be all lies like the rest."

Leo was trying to crawl down off the chair: 'Mum, Mum."

Madam Eva reached him over another biscuit. "If it isn't spirits, what else can it be? Just tell me that."

"I wish I knew. Don't you?"

"It's the spirits all right, don't you fret. Why, what about all those 'undreds of people that talk to their nearest and dearest? They know them, don't they? They know it's them all right. They wouldn't keep on going if they didn't. You can depend on it, if it didn't work there wouldn't be so many doing it."

Jean didn't know what to say to that. She went to take Janet from Madam Eva while she made the tea, but Madam Eva wouldn't let her. "Leave her be, the little sweet."

Jean sat Leo up to the table and cut up his bread and butter for him; and then she told Madam Eva, "Mum says it's only yourself. It's only that when you go off you know things you don't when you're all there."

Madam Eva got quite annoyed over that. "'Ow does she know? She isn't clairvoyante, is she?" She took a sip of tea, and that put her in a good temper again. "Now you listen to me, because I know what I'm talkin' about. I ought to; I've done it the best part of thirty years. And I can tell you," she said, with her finger tapping on the table, "there's more to it than you yourself, whoever you may be. There's something, and I can't tell you what. But everyone knows there is— everyone that does it knows it. There's times there's something tellin' you things—something that isn't you yourself. And if it isn't the spirits, what is it? And some can see them too—I'll say that—some do see them."

Madam Eva stopped to eat, and then she went on again. You can talk about subconscious minds and thought-readin' and such. Those that go in a lot for book-reading can tell you all that. Like Norman Mitch; 'e can talk all that. But don't you believe it; there's something there sometimes, different from others—and everyone that does it knows it."

"He wants me to start Sunday week, the same as before. I can't, can I? I can't do it when I don't know if it's true."

"Haven't I just told you it's true?"

"It isn't true about Daisy. It's all lies."

"Now you oughtn't to go saying that; I do reely think you oughtn't. Just because Norman Mitch 'ad to go talking a lot of rubbish about his sister 'e 'adn't got. When you can help a lot of poor people it's your dooty to do it—that's how I look at it. And you know you can do it, don't you? Well, then."

Jean said, "I can't ever do it if it isn't true."

But Mr. Harsett came in then, and Madam Eva got up to fetch him his tea, with Janet on her arm. Mr. Harsett took notice of her and Leo, and more of Jean than he had all the time she lived there. He sat himself down, and then he said, "Where's Mitch? Is he home yet?"

"Coming next week," Madam Eva told him.

She was bustling round getting his tea. "You won't have room, will you, when 'e's there?" she told Jean. "Better put Leo here, with us, hadn't she? Never 'ave room with Norman and the two of them in that little place."

"That's right, you leave him here."

Jean shook her head. "I'll have room, just the same. He's only coming for the *séance*."

Madam Eva put down the teapot and gave her a dig in the ribs: "Go on, don't you tell me."

"He isn't coming living there," Jean said. "I don't want him." She blushed then, because of Mr. Harsett.

Madam Eva saw it. "Don't you mind him, 'e's no more than your Dad. You take care with Norman, though; you might turn 'im out once too often."

Except for the children it was like old times, sitting there with Mr. Harsett and Madam Eva. Mr. Harsett didn't say any more once he'd taken notice to show he was friendly. Madam Eva kept on about Leo—how she ought to leave him there with them, that it would be easier for her, starting on work again.

But she wouldn't do it. She put his coat on him, and wrapped Janet up in her shawl, and Madam Eva came to the door to help her up the steps with them. "You mind," she told her, "don't go fretting over Daisy. You can depend upon it, whoever she is she wants to be busy 'elping people—even if she isn't Norman Mitch's sister. And no worse for that! Never mind, don't you tell 'im I said it!"

She jumped Leo up the last step and put his hand in Jean's and gave her a poke and a nod. "And mind what I tell you—don't be too hard on 'im."

Jean didn't know what to think. She polished the floor in the big room next day and kept it rubbed up, ready. Only every now and then she'd say, It's lies; I can't do it.

Sometimes while she was rubbing the floor she'd stop a minute and sit up on her heels, looking round the big, empty room, and try to feel if Daisy was there, wanting to talk. Because you do want to be helping people, don't you duck, whoever you are, it's all the same. Because if I was sure you wanted it I'd try, if it was going to help people. Because that's what you want, isn't it, duck. You always did want me to be helping people. Do tell me lovey, tell me you're truly there, and I'll try, reely I will.

But Daisy never said anything.

Even if it isn't her I ought to do it, didn't I?— to help people. That's what Madam Eva said. Even if it's only me and I can help them I ought to. Only I never could do it by myself, I never could lovey, I never could do it if you didn't help me.

Like the old days, when she first started off— trying ever so hard to get off, and never knowing what would come. It was only when you started helping me, duck; I never could do it on my own.

And then when she was getting up in the morning she'd think, It's all lies. I'll tell him I won't do it if he comes in to-day.

But Norman didn't come in, and when it was only four days off she went to see Mum.

"Mum," she asked her—it was what she'd come for—"if it isn't true about the spirits, if it's only yourself, is it wrong doing it to help people?"

Mum told her, "Why don't you leave it alone? It won't do you any good."

"But he wants me to start again, Sunday. Mum, if you're helping people it can't be wrong, is it?"

"You've made your bed," Mum told her, "and you've got to lie on it. I don't hold with it, and I never did. But if you can 'elp people with the Sight that's in you it isn't for me to tell you no— only not for money, mind; you never ought to do it for money."

"I can't help that, Mum; Norman does it. But they're all rich people that come, it doesn't hurt them."

"Rich and foolish," Mum said. "Playing with things that don't concern them. But you must go your own way; you've made your bed, and you must lie on it."

"It can't be wrong helping people, can it, Mum? They're ever so grateful sometimes, some of the private ones; you wouldn't believe."

Mum wouldn't tell her anymore except that she must please herself. She had to get the potatoes peeled for supper, and Jean sat down at the table and gave her a hand. It was funny seeing Leo playing about there in the kitchen again, where she'd played herself when she was a little thing—she and Norah and Joyce and Tom. They'd all gone off now. And Mum was getting old, but she didn't mind having Leo playing round; she said it livened the old place up.

He was running about, tumbling over the bumps in the floor. Jean dropped a peel down and told him, "There, Lee-o, run and put it in the rubbish box, there's a good boy."

She watched him toddling off, falling over the rocker of Dad's chair, round the corner of the dresser to the back kitchen where the floor was more bumpy still. It used to be ever such a long journey. And Janet was put to sleep on the old sofa, where they used to play about.

When she was putting on Leo's coat it crossed her mind, I might leave him here. But she thought, No I won't though. I'd miss him.

Dad came in just when she was going, and asked if Norman was back yet. She said he had been, and she was going to start work in a day or two; and Dad said, "That's right."

When she'd got home and put Janet and Leo to bed she suddenly thought how she'd told Dad she was going to start on with the *séances* again. And then she thought how Mum had said she ought to if it could help people. So she really would have to try. You are there, Daisy duck, you will help me, won't you. I never could do it without you.

Norman came back on the Saturday. He took a look round the front room to see it was all right, and got out his velvet coat and brushed it. He'd had his hair cut, and the piece that was left long was sleeked over the bald patch with brilliantine.

He didn't ask Jean if she meant to do it, and she didn't tell him anything. I'll try, Daisy duck, she said, giving Janet her bottle and settling her down. I'll try, if you'll help me.

Leo stared at Norman, sitting there at tea-time, and Norman told him to mind his manners and not stare at people.

Leo wasn't used to that after Norman playing with him, and it made him start to cry.

Norman said, "For God's sake, is that the way you bring him up? The boy wants a good leathering."

He didn't touch him, though, and Jean made Leo quiet down and finish up his tea.

While she was putting him to bed Norman looked up from his paper he was reading and said something, but she didn't hear what.

"There, be good boy, Lee-o, go to sleep."

She came back to the table. Norman said, "What the devil have you got him back here for? He ought to be with your people."

"He was there till a few weeks ago," she told him quickly.

"Well, he'd better get back there."

"Mum can't keep him forever." She started piling up the plates.

Norman slammed down his paper. "I see. So I can get out again. That's it, is it?"

She didn't say anything.

He jumped up and put on his coat and hat. "I've put up with more from you," he said, "than any mortal man would."

He slammed the door when he went out.

He was back the next day an hour before the *séance*, with his soft voice on and his velvet coat and his hair sleeked down, giving the room a look round and showing up the people.

He took Leo to the lady downstairs. Janet was having her afternoon sleep; she didn't wake up as a rule till getting on for five.

Jean brushed the blue velvet dress and put it on; it hung on her. Funny I haven't got any bigger, with having two of them. She wondered about it for a bit while she plaited her hair and twisted it round her head, and then she remembered what she'd got to do: go in there and go off. She felt dead and dull. She could hear Norman outside: "This way, if you please, my dear lady. This way, if you please."

You'll come, won't you, Daisy, if you're there. And if you aren't he'll know then.

He came to fetch her. "Full house," he muttered, and she went in ahead of him into the big room. All the chairs were full; she could see the room full of people's backs, and some of their faces when she came alongside. The light shone on some of them from behind her empty chair. She didn't recognize any; they were just people—ladies and gentlemen; all quiet, waiting for her.

She got frightened then. Daisy, Daisy, do help me, there's a dear.

She passed the front row and went to her chair and sat down. Her knees were shaking. They were all looking at her. She remembered then, and shut her eyes. She heard Norman start: "Ladies—and—gentlemen. There is no one present to-day who will not learn with profound pleasure that Madam Jan, the world-famous trance medium, has returned from her travels and…"

Even that's lies, she thought.

"… is here once more to bring to you the little spirit-child Daisy."

Why does he talk with that silly voice. Why can't he say it like he does when he goes on at me: Blast you, shut your blasted mouth, how the hell do I know…?

"This little girl, who left this earth of ours more than twenty years ago and now dwells in the changeless world of spirits…"

And he doesn't even believe in it.

"…is with us here to-day, ready and eager as she ever was to help you talk with your loved ones." He paused, and went on again. "The one thing she is anxious to do…"

Suddenly Jean felt the sweat break out. Daisy, now. I've got to do it now. Daisy do help me, do, do, help me Daisy.

"…ready and anxious, is to bring joy and comfort to us who still dwell upon this sad earth…"

Daisy, please, Daisy, do come, please, Daisy.

She lowered her head. She could feel the sweat breaking out on her forehead.

"…by bringing to our midst the dear ones who are no longer present in the flesh."

He paused, and she heard him move nearer. He jogged her shoulder; he must have done it as if it was an accident.

"As she comes among us to-day we feel around us the presence of the Great Unseen..."

Daisy, I must, I must, now.

Her mouth was open. She heard herself say, "Hallo, every..." And then it stopped. It wasn't—it was me; I only said it myself.

Norman had stopped talking. There wasn't a sound in the room. She whispered, "I can't."

She didn't dare to look. She sat there with her eyes shut. She whispered, "I can't do it."

Norman moved suddenly, in going forward he gave her a push that sent her sideways in the chair. He was standing in front of her. "Ladies and gentlemen, I very much regret that the medium has been taken ill and the *séance* cannot take place this afternoon." She heard him draw in his breath.

She covered her eyes with her hand. They all began to whisper and then to talk in low voices. Nobody moved; they didn't know what they were expected to do. Then she heard one of them say, quite plain, "Do they return the money?"

Norman must have heard it too. He said—what had he been doing, just standing there?—"Ladies and gentlemen, the tickets will be available at a later date, to be announced."

Then he went away, towards the door, and they began to push back their chairs and get up. "This way, ladies and gentlemen, if you please, this way."

When she opened her eyes they had all gone. The chairs were standing empty in until y rows. All the lights were on. The door was open, and Norman was still talking outside—that must be the last one. "I can't tell you, my dear lady, how sorry I am..."

His voice went away down the stairs.

So you aren't there, Daisy duck. You aren't, after all.

She sat still, listening for him to come back. He'd swear at her worse than ever now; he'd say she did it on purpose. I didn't though, duck, I did try. I'd have done it if you'd wanted to.

She sat still, waiting dully for him to come and swear at her and get it over.

He was coming up the stairs, and she could feel her heart beating faster. She was afraid of what he'd say to her, even though she didn't care. I don't care, I can't help it, I can't do it, it's lies. She gripped the arms of the chair; her hands were cold and sweaty.

He went into the back room. He was taking off his coat. He wasn't coming in then, he was going. He'd go, he wouldn't come back, he wouldn't come anymore.

He was opening his case and throwing things in. She moved, and found out how cramped she was. She kicked the long skirt away from round her feet. As soon as he'd gone she ought to go in and see to Janet. He was coming out across the landing; her heart missed a beat and went on quicker. He came into the room and switched the lights off. In the half-dark he went across and drew back the curtains, letting in daylight over the untidy chairs. He didn't say anything. He wasn't going to say anything. He was only going.

He came back past her, pushing a chair out of his way. He stopped and stood in front of her and looked at her, but he didn't say anything. Then he smacked her across the face.

When he'd gone she went on sitting there, in the daylight, in front of the empty pushed-about chairs. She only thought, It's finished, I haven't got to do it anymore. He had left the door open, and presently she heard Janet crying in the other room. She got up then and went to her. "What is it then, Jan-it?"

She put the bottle to warm on the stove and took off the blue velvet dress. When it was off she stood holding it for a minute, then suddenly she rolled it in a ball and threw it into the corner. She went back and picked up Janet and quieted her and gave her her bottle. Then she just sat, with Janet gone to sleep in her arms, and stared in front of her.

When it began to get dark she put Janet in the cot and got into her everyday clothes, her old skirt and cardigan with the dragged-down pockets, and picked up the blue dress and hung it behind the curtain. I shan't ever wear that one anymore. Then she fetched Leo from downstairs.

She sat him up to the table and gave him his tea. But he wouldn't eat. He kept waving his spoon out of the plate, looking round between mouthfuls.

"Eat up, Lee-o."

"Where's the man?"

"Gone away," she told him.

She sat up till past ten, afraid Norman might come back. He won't, though. We won't see any more of him now. He won't come back here again.

So there wasn't anything. There isn't anything, after all.

She couldn't get to sleep for hours that night; her eyes were wide open. It kept going round in her mind: the *séance* and the people sitting there waiting, and Norman, and then when he came back...

She got up and looked out of the window into the dark. I won't have him here, she thought. No I won't, I won't have him. I won't.

It woke Leo up, getting cold by himself, and she had to get in again and hold him, "What is it, Lee-o? Go to sleep." Trying to go off, and the people waiting, and then Norman...

She dug her face in the back of Leo's head. I hate 'im, yes I do. I hate 'im.

"There, go to sleep, lovey."

Next day she went in to tidy up the front room, the door was still open and the chairs standing about. She dusted them and stood them back straight round the walls. She felt like stone. One of the ladies had dropped a handkerchief—chiffon, with marks of lipstick on it. She put it on a chair by the door in case it was asked for. She ran the mop over the floor and then shut the door and turned the key.

She didn't go in there again.

She didn't see anyone for nearly a week. saw to the children, and took them out the once or twice she had to go to the shops. When they got back she just sat and sewed while Leo played about, or sat and looked in front of her. Until Leo said something—"Mum, Mum"—and then she answered him and took up her sewing again.

Then Madam Eva called in, ever so flustered. "Whatever did you do it for, to upset 'im like that"

Jean just looked at her. "You saw him, then?"

"Saw 'im? I should think I did see 'im. Whatever did you do that for? You oughtn't to've done that, letting him down in front of all the clients. He's got a lot of faith in you, Norman Mitch has—did have, any'ow. You oughtn't to've let 'im down like that."

She sat back and looked round, snapping her fingers to make Leo come to her. It made her all flustered, Jean sitting there so quiet, looking at her without saying anything.

Jean asked her at last, "Does he believe in his own job?"

That took Madam Eva aback too. "He's a clever man," she told her, watching her, not sure what she wanted her to say. "He's a fine astrologer, Norman Mitch is. 'E's got a good connexion too. But natchrally no one likes bein' made a fool of, do they, in front of people?"

Jean looked at her for a minute; she was twisted right round, reaching out after Leo. "What did you come here for? Did he send you?"

Madam Eva twisted back quick. "Bless you, he wouldn't send me! Aren't you queer? I only wondered.... Did 'e leave you any money in the house? See here, I'll give you some and get it from im. 'E can't go off leaving you like that."

Jean pushed it back. "I don't want his money—and I don't want him."

Madam Eva had her mouth open. "Whatever will you do, then?"

"I don't care. I don't know. Go out to work."

Madam Eva pushed it back. "Go on, you can't let the kiddies starve, can you?"

Jean looked at it as if she'd push it back again, but she left it there.

"Tell you what I'd do," Madam Eva told her.

"I'd work up a little business of your own, with cards and crystal. I might be able to pass you on a client or two to get you started. You'd soon work up a connexion, even if you didn't get the same smart lot. Get a few regulars to keep you going."

Jean jumped up then. "No, I won't. I won't have any more to do with it. If I work I'll do it honest. I've done with all that, and I've done with him."

"You can't be done with both," Madam Eva told her, getting rattled. "What're you goin' to live on?"

"I don't know, and I don't care."

"You're a fool," Madam Eva told her, puffing and fanning herself. "Talking about dishonest! That isn't the way to talk. Not honest, isn't it? You'll be telling me I'm not honest, next."

"You may be. I don't know, and I don't care." Jean wouldn't look at her anymore; she looked out of the window. "I'm not having any of it, and I'm not having any of him either."

Madam Eva got up. "You'll be telling a different tale before you're much older—quarrelling with your bread and butter! You'll be coming round on your bended knees askin' me to find you clients before you've done."

"I don't want to quarrel with you," Jean said dully. "Only I don't want any more to do with it— nor with him."

"As you like. You'll soon be singin' a different tune."

Madam Eva went away, huffy.

When she'd gone Jean saw the money was still on the table. She looked at it as if she'd like to throw it out of the window. Only there was Leo and Janet. She fetched her shabby purse from the pocket of her coat. There was fivepence in it. She slipped in

Madam Eva's money and pushed the purse back into the pocket and humped up her shoulders. That's the last, though. I'll go out to work.

The next day while she was getting Leo ready to go out she heard him on the stairs, and in a minute he was inside the room.

She didn't look up. She'd sat Leo on the side of the bed and she was kneeling down buttoning up his gaiters. Norman was there in front of her, but she didn't look to see what he was doing. She could feel the blood heating in her ears with hating him, wanting to turn him out. She gave Leo a pull to stop him looking round.

Norman didn't say anything.

When she'd buttoned up the two gaiters she couldn't stay down there any longer. She got up suddenly. Get out, she said in her mind. Her heart was pounding; it made her feel sick. She stood straight and looked at him.

"Come here," he told her.

She took a step forward. He was just standing, waiting for her. She stopped; she couldn't go on.

He put his case on the table and opened it.

"Come here."

She went on slowly until she was standing in front of him, by the table. He was looking in his case; he didn't take any notice of her having come. She watched him turning over the books and papers.

He didn't say anything.

She said suddenly, in a gasp, "I don't care. If you want to hit me you can."

"Don't be a bloody fool," he said.

She swayed. Why doesn't he, I wish he did.

She stood with head down, watching him.

"Norman."

In the same moment he found what he was looking for, and held it out to her. "Here, you'd better pack up and be ready to move in two days. I can't afford to keep up this expensive place for nothing. You can get on with that, and earn your keep."

She stared at him.

"Read it, you fool."

She looked at it. It was a visiting-card with "Madame Jeanne" on it, and an address. It said underneath: "Palmistry and Psychology. Trance sittings by appointment."

She said faintly, "I can't do it, Norman."

He snapped his case to and picked up his hat. "You'll damn' well do what I tell you to."

G

Up the dusty stairs between Guinea Gowns and Off Licence. ORIGI-
NAL GIPSY BETH; third floor. "That's right, come along in. I c'n tell
yer something will 'elp you, I c'n see I can."

Gipsy Beth is an old woman. She has a dirty red handkerchief
tied gipsy fashion round her neck over her dirty, ordinary clothes.

"Come along in, that's right." She sidles round and shuts the door.
"Now what'll you 'ave, dear? Two-'n-six, five shilling...?"

The window is tight shut; you can hear the buses rumbling down
below. Two flies are crawling on the window-pane.

"I'll try the two-and-six, if you don't mind."

"Put it on yer 'and."

She takes the money and draws a cross with it. "Cross yer palm
with silver, that's for luck." There is black under her nails. She slips
the coin away quickly in a pocket of her skirt.

"Now I c'n see a man, jus' round the corner from you. In... You
ever worked in an office?"

"Well, I do, reely."

"*That's right, that would be it. There's this man, I see 'im in an office.... Got any more money, dear?*"

"*No, not reely.*"

"*It takes a lot of seein', this does. Now, come along, dear, I c'n 'elp you, reely I can. I c'n see big things comin' for yer, only jus' round the corner. I like you, 'n' I'd like to 'elp yer, 'n' I don't say that to everyone, mind. But there's somethin' about you makes me feel I c'n 'elp yer. An' I c'n see there's a lot comin' for yer.... Come along, dear. There's a pound note you got in your bag, I c'n see it.*"

"*But I can't give you that, reely. Can't I just have the two-and-six one?*"

"*Come on, now, it'll be worth yer while. With all that's comin', like I c'n see it.*"

"*But I can't, reely. I've got to do the shopping going home, reely I have.*"

"*I'll tell yer what it is—there's a big opportunity comin' to yer. Only jus' roun' the corner, I c'n see it. Now do you know what I'd like? I'd like to get the crystal onter this. It's worth it, mind. It isn't often I see someone come in 'ere with a bit er luck waitin' for them the way you got. Now I'll tell you what I'll do—an' it's what I wouldn't do for every one: It's a pound the crystal, but I'll do it for you for ten bob. There now !*"

"*But I'll have to go, reely. Oh, all right. Well, look here. Here's half a crown more I could let you have. Tell me just that bit .. . *"

Gipsy Beth claws up the coin and puts it into her skirt. "*Well, I think yer wrong, really you are. I c'd 'elp yer, mind, if I c'd get the crystal onter this. An' a big opportunity I c'n see for yer...*"

"*But that bit about that man? Just tell me that.*"

"*Well, there yer are. I c'd see it all clear if yer'd only let me...*"

"*But I'll have to go, reely.*"

"*Come on, dear. Give us another 'alf crown 'n' I'll tell yer some more.*"

VIII

Madam Eva took a look round the sitting-room. "So you've come to it, like the rest of us. No more stujios with paintin's on the wall—always did give me the creeps. I daresay you'd as soon be without, wouldn't you?"

There was hardly anything in the sitting-room. Only a divan Norman picked up second-hand, with an oriental rug over it, and a table put out in the middle with a chair each side, for Jean and a client. Outside the window you could see a bit of grass and a privet hedge that hid people half-way up when they went by in the street.

Madam Eva was still a bit huffy over what Jean said to her the last time, but she couldn't keep it up once she got her cup of tea. "It's a cosy little place you got, reely. A bit out of the way. But I daresay you'll do a good bit local."

Jean said, "He might as well have gone out to Edenfields while we were about it, or High Lanes anyhow, then I'd have been nearer Mum. He doesn't like Mum, though."

"Ar, she tells 'im off, I expect."

"She never said anything to him. He just doesn't like her."

"Well, you can't have everything, can you? So 'e's gone off again?"

"He came for the move. And then he said he'll be back later on."

"Ar. Well you're better off here, aren't you?"

Leo woke up then, and called out. He was getting big to sleep in the afternoons. Jean went in and fetched him, and when Madam Eva had done her tea she took her in to look at Janet sleeping in the bedroom behind.

"Dear little thing. She is growing, isn't she?" She took a look round. "So you've got a kitchen too, this time? Better off, aren't you?"

Jean didn't say anything to that. She showed Madam Eva the kitchen out at the back, which was big enough for them to eat in, and the bit of yard.

"More like my place, isn't it?—only not downstairs. You'll be a lot better off here. Got your plate up, I see."

There were two bells by the front door, the upstairs and theirs. Theirs had MITCH by it, and underneath, smaller: "Madame Jeanne, Palmistry, Psychology."

Jean nodded. She did hope nobody'd ever come. There wasn't any reason why they should; you couldn't read the plate from out in the street. She said good-bye, and watched Madam Eva go bobbing off along outside the privet hedge, to the corner, where the trams ran by.

Norman came back two or three days later; she didn't know whether she wanted him to or not. He came back and brought his suit-case with him, so he meant to stop. When she went to put Leo to bed after tea Norman looked up and said she could put him to sleep on the divan in the sitting-room. She didn't know even then whether she was sorry. She was only thinking of how Leo might get frightened, all by himself. She drew the curtains back so that he could see the lights out in the street, and left the door open.

She really couldn't have said if she was sorry or if she wasn't that Norman had come back. He wasn't nice to her like he used to be, hardly ever; it was as if he wanted to have her frightened of him, and the same with the children. When he went off, as he did very soon, saying he had to go on a business trip that might take some time, she was downright glad for a bit, being alone with them again. And then after a few days she was missing him.

Sometimes she'd think, I hate him, I hope he doesn't ever come back. And then she'd hug up Leo and say, "There, be good boy, Lee-o. Don't ever be like Dad, will you, Lee-o?"

Then when he did come back he only looked in a minute and was going out again. But she went over and stood by him and said, "Norman," ever so quiet, so she could hardly hear it herself, even. And then he gave a smile to himself, and stayed a day or two. He was like that—he never called her; he always made her come of her own accord. It was what made her hate him in a way.

It was one day while he was there, but gone out to business, that she got her first client. She went to answer the door, and it never entered her head it might be anything. There was a girl standing there, and she said, "Are you Madam Jean?"

Jean said, "Yes," and she went on waiting; she never thought.

The girl came up closer and spoke quiet, as if someone was going to hear. "I saw the advert," she said. "I couldn't make an appointment. Can I come in now, or have you got someone?"

Jean felt herself go hot. So he was advertising, and she there hoping no one would see the name on the bell. Trust Norman. "You can come in if you like." She pushed the sitting-room door. She was wondering, Will I ever remember, cards and all of it? She looked fierce at the client's back. I won't do the other though, no I won't.

She sat down at the table and the client sat down at the other side. She wasn't so young as all that when you looked at her close. She said, "I'll have the half-crown one, if you don't mind—the palmistry."

She spread her hands out; they were red and chilblained, not as if she did housework, though. Might be a shopgirl, out of a job. Jean started reading off the lines. "You let your heart rule your head, don't you?" She had a cheap ring on her engagement finger. "You'll be getting married soon now."

She did it all like Madam Eva taught her, like saying off a lesson. It couldn't be wrong, what was written in all the books, that any-one could read if they liked. It wasn't like telling about the spirits.

She said it off as quick as she could, trying to listen what Leo and Janet were doing out at the back.

When she'd done the girl asked her, "And will I get my job back?"

"You won't want it, will you, if you're getting married?"

But she didn't look sure. Jean told her, "You can have a wish with the cards, if you like," and she brightened up.

Jean got up to fetch the cards from where he he'd put them on the mantelpiece. She could always remember that one, the wish: the aces and the rest.

"Is that extra, though?"

She looked so anxious Jean couldn't help smiling.

"You can have that thrown in, just the wish."

She watched her shuffle—you could see she wasn't used to it. "And cut with your left hand."

They didn't all come up, but Jean couldn't bear to disappoint her. "You'll get it all right if you wait," she told her. "You'll have to wait, though." It must mean that. And mostly you did get things if you waited long enough.

When the girl went away she said, "There's someone I know might want to come some time."

Jean smiled—not that she wanted any more; but it was nice of her thinking of it.

She put the half-crown on the kitchen-table, and when Norman came in she told him, "I had one here to-day—a client."

He picked it up. "What—is that all?" He looked at her, suspicious.

"I thought you'd put it in the paper how much it was. She seemed as if she knew."

"What did she have? Palmistry?"

"That's all."

"Palmistry two-and-six, cartomancy two-and-six, psychology two-and-six. You've got to tot it up to seven-and-six, my girl—at the very least."

"But suppose they won't have more than one?"

"Then you've got to work it—that's your job. And don't forget, astrology to order. That's mine. Take down their name and address, age, date of birth, time if known. And jot down anything that might come in handy."

"I will if they want it."

"Want be damned! You've got to make them want it."

He looked at her sour all that evening. But she didn't care. She hoped there wouldn't be any more coming.

Two days later there was another one. And after her reading she said, "Can I have the wish? For the same?"

You could see the other one must have told her.

Jean let her have it; she wasn't going to tell Norman.

It didn't come out any better for her than for the first, but it seemed a shame to say it. You couldn't have the heart to when they looked at you like that. "You'll get it all right," she to her. "You wait a bit." Anyhow, she thought, I'm not charging her for it.

After that there were quite a few. They hardly ever rang up—just came to the door. She got know the likely times, and when the bell rang she put Leo and Janet out in the yard if it was fine, where they couldn't fall on the fire or hurt themselves; or shut them in the bedroom if it was wet.

And then she hadn't got to listen so hard while she read their hands or laid the cards out; because they didn't like it, sitting with the door open, most of them. Had the feeling someone was going to hear. She always gave them the wish thrown in if they wanted it.

Some that were better off asked for the two right away, and then she had five shillings to give Norman to put him in a good temper. But she never tried to push them to it, until one time months later, when it was near Christmas and she wanted a Christmas present for Janet.

Norman was always ready to give Leo things, but he hardly took any notice of Janet—anything was good enough for her. One day when Jean took her out there was a lovely dollie in a window, with real hair on, and Janet kept looking, saying, "Mum, Mum, dollie!"

It was a dear little dollie with yellow curls and blue eyes, and Jean wanted ever so to give her Janet.

And then one afternoon the bell rang, and it was a lady, quite smart. "Perhaps I ought to have made an appointment," she said. "I wonder Madam Jeanne could see me?"

Jean told her to come in.

"Oh, *you're* Madame Jeanne?" She looked a bit as if she didn't believe it.

"What will you have?" Jean asked her.

"I should like to have my hand read, I think."

She looked ever so rich, and Jean suddenly thought of it: "You get better results if you have the cards too—and psychology," she said quickly. "That comes to seven-and-six."

"Oh, I see. Very well, you can give me all of them."

Jean was quite in a tremble while she laid out the cards. She didn't know quite herself what the psychology was, or where you put it. Madam Eva used to say it came in when you looked at a client extra careful, and then you must ask their birth date and tell them what their lucky days were. "Why," she said, "the sixteenth is your lucky date, that's to-day." Must be a lucky one for me too, she thought.

The lady put down the seven-and-six without so much as a murmur; the sort that would have handed over a guinea or more up in the West End. Wonder whatever brought her here. You never know, though. Wanted to go where she wasn't known, very likely.

"I'll give you my card," Jean told her, flushing a bit. It was the first time she'd ever given one. She took it from the pile Norman had put behind the clock months ago, and watched the lady slip it into her bag.

"You don't do astrology?" the lady asked her.

"No-er—my husband does, though. He's a professor."

"Oh, really? How interesting! I may want a horoscope cast another day."

The lady went off. Jean put one of the half-crowns on the kitchen-table and the other two in her pocket for Janet. After all, she's got a right to it, poor little mite.

When Norman came in she told him, "There was one here to-day asking about astrology. The first that ever has."

"Right. Got the particulars?"

"She didn't want it now, only to know."

He picked up the half-crown. "Is that all she had besides? Well, you've got her name and address all right?"

"She didn't give it to me."

"What! So you're too much of a fool even to do that."

"She said she'd come back, reely she did."

He shrugged angrily and turned his back on her.

She didn't care if Norman thought she was a fool. She got the dollie for Janet; she was ever so sweet with it. Janet was a funny little thing now she was bigger—with a thin little face, and dark hair that grew down over, and Jean cut it in a fringe. She looked like a little gipsy. Jean could have watched her for hours playing with her dollie. It was while she was watching her she suddenly thought what the dollie looked like; it was the very spit of Daisy.

"What're you going to call her then, Jan-it?"

"Don't know."

"Why don't you call her Daisy? She's ever so like a little girl I used to know was called Daisy."

Janet called her Daisy then, and she'd sit talking to Daisy in a corner, by the hour sometimes.

It was the funniest thing to hear her. Jean had such a funny feeling now about Daisy—the real Daisy—as if she was someone she used to know that had died. When she heard Janet going on Daisy this and Daisy that she'd think, You don't mind, do you, lovey? But it wasn't like someone alive she was talking to; it was like to the memory of her.

"Mum," Janet would say. "Mum."

"What is it, my duck?"

"Mum, Daisy's hungry now. Daisy wants her tea and go to bed."

And then she'd take her in with her and hug her up, for all the world as if it was someone alive.

Once she did it in front of Norman: "Mum, Daisy get up now."

And Norman jumped round as if you'd shot him. "What the devil?"

Jean's heart came into her mouth. "It's only her dollie," she told him quickly. And then she was afraid again, in case he should ask where she got it from.

But he only gave a hard stare at Janet and her dollie and shrugged his shoulders. He didn't think of it.

Jean didn't know till then what she was afraid of. She took to watching Janet after that, but she never could make out what she was telling to Daisy, all by herself. Jean got the old mailcart from home now Janet was big enough and they lived on the ground floor. She could push Janet in it, with her Daisy hugged up in her arms, and Leo was old enough to walk alongside without getting tired and wanting to be picked up. He was growing a big boy now, soon be going to school. She had to put him out in the yard to play when she had a client, so that he shouldn't make a noise or go teasing Janet. He was big enough now to be rough with her.

One day the bell rang and she pushed him outside the back and shut Janet in the bedroom with her dollie, and it was an elderly woman; she didn't often get them. Not very well-off looking, but as if she'd have the five shillings most likely.

Jean took her in the sitting-room and got her sat down, and then just when Jean was going for the cards she leaned over and told her, whispering almost, "I want trance."

It made Jean turn all funny; she couldn't think of an answer for a minute. Then she remembered: "You'll have to make an appointment for that. I'm sorry," she said, for the old thing looked so disappointed.

"Oh, go on, you can do it now, can't you? I don't mind waiting."

"I'm ever so sorry."

"Oh go on, I'll tell you how it is. It's my Billy—'e was killed sudden two months back, away at his work, and never left no wishes nor anything, and it preys on my mind so, to think if there was anything 'e wanted. You know, if there was anything 'e wanted done...."

Jean said, "Oo, I do wish I could help you." She was like that—when someone wanted helping she couldn't hold out. Daisy duck, could I do it do you think?

"Oh go on, you can do it to-day 's well as any other, can't you?"

"I'll have a try," Jean said. As soon as she'd said it she'd have given anything not to have done. Whatever will I do if I can't go off. You help me duck, you know you can, you're there aren't you, when anyone wants helping.

The client was sitting looking at her with her eyes wide open, waiting for her to do something.

"You just sit quiet and wait," Jean told her. "I'll do it if can. If I can't it's because you got to have time beforehand, getting ready." She won't know any different.

"That's right, Mrs.," the woman told her, "you take your time. I'm not in any 'urry."

Jean shut her eyes and tried as hard as ever she could to see Daisy there in front of her, and she hadn't seen her so clear for years. You help me, duck. Come on, do help me.

The next thing she knew she heard Daisy say, "Hallo, every-one!" And then she was coming round, and the old woman was wiping her eyes there across the table. Jean couldn't think for a minute where she was.

"Wasn't that lovely now? 'Im saying 'e was so 'appy over there. An' all about 'ow it is—it does your 'eart good to 'ear 'im. To think of my Billy…"

She went on wiping her eyes, and then she looked up, fright-ened all at once. "Is that very dear? I never thought to ask."

"You can have it for the five shillings," Jean told her. It was all Norman would look for.

She was ever so grateful. She went out saying how it was won-derful and how it put new heart into her.

"Don't send any more, though," Jean told her on the door-step—"not for that. I can't often do it."

"Ar, it must wear you out. Yes, I can see it does."

Thank you, Daisy love. I won't do it anymore, though—not more than I can help. It can't be wrong, though, can it, when it does good to someone like that?

She felt tired right out. She went in and took Janet on her lap and sat there quiet, with Janet babbling away about her Daisy. Jean couldn't help a smile. You don't mind, do you lovey? Outside in the yard Leo was playing drums, banging a tin tray on the dustbin.

After a bit she went to the window and told him, "Do stop it, Lee-o."

But he wouldn't leave off all at once, and when he did he started sulking. He was getting ever so noisy and bad-tempered; it was time he was going to school. It was the way Norman went on with him—one time cuffing him for nothing, and another time letting him do what he liked, giving him sweets and money. Everything with Norman was just according to how he felt. Leo was ever so much better behaved when Norman went away for a week or two, which he did off and on.

She never said anything to Norman about her having gone off that time in a sitting, or he'd have been at her again to go on with it regular. And she didn't want to be doing it. She hardly got anyone for trance, anyhow, not once in six months. Ten shillings was what he'd told her to charge, and there weren't many people round here who'd spend that much. The next one she got she did charge it to, for she didn't want her going away sending others; she didn't want it going round that she'd do it cheap. She had ever such a job getting off too that time. Daisy duck, do help me, do. But she never talked to Daisy now except when she wanted her, and p'raps that was why she wouldn't come.

She had ever such a job to get her to do it, and it was a near thing. She thought to herself, I'll start off talking, the way he used to; it might help me to go off. And if she wants to come she will, and if not I'll say I can't do it.

She started off saying slowly, "I see the lovely spirit-world. I see all the lovely spirits coming round—coming to help you."

She went on a bit, and then it was as if her voice faded off in the distance, and Daisy must have taken over, because the next she knew she was coming round again and the client seemed satisfied.

She thought to herself, I don't care with this sort if I have to say I can't do it. It isn't like in a *séance*.

But she was glad they didn't keep on coming; she couldn't have kept on with it. Only it was lucky for her in a way when she did get one because since she didn't want to say it to Norman she had the money for herself, to spend on Janet.

She had Janet to herself more, now Leo was starting school. When she'd got them up in the morning and given Norman his breakfast if he was there, she sat Janet in the mailcart and did up the strap over her and wheeled her out to take Leo to school. He used to walk alongside quiet enough for a bit, till they saw any of the others going, the rough ones that were let to go by themselves, and then he'd want to run off after them and she had to hold on to him. Then he'd kick at the wheels of the mailcart to try and make Janet cry, but she wouldn't; she'd be good as gold.

"Be good boy now, Lee-o," Jean would tell him, sending him in through the Infants' door. And he'd run off in without even waving back to her.

Then Jean would wheel Janet home and let her play round her while she did her work, and listen to her talking to her Daisy dollie and making up games to herself. Sometimes she said things that made Jean wonder, only she told herself it was only her fancy—like about the big bears that came and climbed up the window, that she and Daisy knew all about. They all make up tales to themselves, though—all babies do, don't they.

Sometimes she wouldn't bother to listen, and very often she had to leave Janet by herself while she went in to see a client. And then she put her in the cart and wheeled her out again to fetch Leo back from school.

Once he'd got out of the "Infants" into the "Boys" he wouldn't go with her anymore. He ran off as soon as they got in the road near the school, and wouldn't come when she told him.

"Come here, you naughty boy. Lee-o!"

But he only put his tongue out at her and ran off with the others.

Janet was walking now, part of the way, pushing the cart along with Jean. But Jean couldn't leave her to run after Leo, so she had to let him go.

She told Norman about it, but Norman wouldn't stop him. "Let him go. He doesn't want you, tying him on to your apron-strings. Let the boy alone, to find his own feet."

So she didn't take him to school anymore. She and Janet went out on their own later on in the morning to do the shopping.

And then one day when they were coming back Janet suddenly looked up at her and asked her, "Mum, what is it makes things come when you go to sleep?"

Jean felt as if her heart had stood still. She half stopped, but

Janet tugged her on. "What does, my duck?"

"Like pictures that you see, when you shut your eyes up tight."

"It's only dreams," she said. She felt as if she'd faint in a minute. "Don't take any notice of it, lovey; it's only dreams."

"No, it isn't. Reely, Mum. Dreams is when you're asleep, but this is diff'rent; it's when you shut your eyes up tight—or when you don't sometimes, but it's dark."

"It isn't anything," she said thickly. She didn't know till then how much she'd always been afraid.

"But it is, Mum. Mum, what is it?"

"I don't know, my duck. But don't say it to anyone, ever. Don't ever say it to Dad."

"Why not, Mum?"

Jean squeezed her hand tighter; she didn't know how to make her not say it. "You never tell secrets to anyone, do you? It's a secret you and me have got."

Janet nodded, as solemn as anything. She wouldn't tell it to him now.

She never would, though—not on purpose. She was frightened of him, even though he didn't go on at her like he did at Leo. He never took any notice of her except to say, "Shut up!" sometimes, when she was talking.

He was awful with Leo. Once he told him something and Leo put his tongue out at him. He'd often done it at her and Norman hadn't said anything. But this time he went red as fire and then dead-white, and said, "Come here."

It was in the kitchen, and Leo put his tongue out at him again and ran out into the yard.

Norman went to the door and told him, "Come here," as if he was a dog, and started taking his belt off.

Leo didn't take any notice at first; he only ran off further. But he couldn't get out of the yard, and Norman was standing in the door, with the belt in his hand, telling him, "Come here."

He had to come. He couldn't help it.

Jean couldn't see from where she was. She could only see Norman standing in the door, in his shirt-sleeves, with the sun shining down on his bald head. And then when she moved round there was Leo creeping up to him along by the wall, as if he was too terrified to move almost, and when he got close he stood still and cried and put his arm up over his eyes.

She couldn't bear it anymore. She caught hold of Norman's arm. "Don't hit him, Norman; don't."

"Don't be a bloody fool," he told her.

He turned round then and came in and threw his belt on a chair, and she saw he was smiling to himself to think how he'd frightened her. Then he picked up the belt and put it on again.

She didn't see what Leo was doing out in the yard, but after a bit he came in, looking scared to death, and Norman didn't take any more notice of him.

He was cowed the rest of that day, but the next day he was worse than ever. He came home from school kicking his football into the house, all over mud, and knocked into Janet and made her fall down. When he saw Norman was there he stopped and went quite white.

Jean told him, "Lee-o, you naughty boy!"

But Norman only said he'd got to learn to be a man, and called him and gave him a shilling.

Leo didn't like him any more for it, though. He was frightened of him, the same as Janet. And now Norman had found out he could frighten Jean he used to do it just for that; pretending he was going to hit Leo, and then not doing it. It only made Leo worse when he wasn't there.

And yet he used to pamper him. With Janet getting bigger Norman got a camp-bed and put it in the kitchen, and Jean said Leo could sleep there and Janet could have the divan in the sitting-room. But Norman said he should stay where he was, and

Janet could sleep in the kitchen.

Janet was going to school now. Jean took her along in the mornings. Sometimes they'd see Leo in the distance, running off, or having a scrap with another boy. When they got to the gate of the playground Jean would tell her, "Bye-bye, Jan-it; be good girl now!" Not that she ever was anything but good, bless her little heart.

And Janet would keep on turning round and waving back to her. "Tat-ta, Mum. Tat-ta!"

The house seemed ever so empty without her.

Even when Janet got bigger, and was in among the big girls, Jean would go part way with her, for company, and do her shopping on the way home. She wanted Janet to have her own friends, though; she never interfered with her, even if she didn't come straight back after school. But Janet never stopped about till late, not like Leo. She'd come in and help her Mum get the tea, and later on Jean would come and tuck her in her little bed in the kitchen and tell her good-night. When Norman wasn't there she had her in with her, and hugged her up and told her to be a good girl and not stay awake making up stories.

One night when Janet was nearly eight, getting a big girl, she woke Jean up in the middle of the night and gave her quite a turn. "Mum, Granny's been 'ere. She was here just now."

Jean told her to go to sleep and not go imagining things. But she couldn't get to sleep herself after that for wondering about it. And then the next morning she got the wire saying Mum had passed away.

"And to think you saw her, Jan-it, and I never did."

She was upset about it both ways. To think she never saw Mum when she came to say good-bye. And that showed there were spirits, didn't it? That just showed. It was as if Mum came to tell her, so she'd be sure. And then to think of Janet seeing her... "Don't you ever tell it to Dad, mind, will you lovey."

Madam Eva came when she heard about Mum. She didn't

often come nowadays; she was getting on, and it was a long way for her. "Dear, dear. There, to think of her passing over."

Madam Eva wasn't her old self, time was telling on her. She kept saying it wouldn't be long now before she passed over too; it was as much as she could do to keep about and see clients. Jean asked her why she didn't retire; but she said no, she wouldn't do that, she'd die in harness the way she lived.

Janet came home from school while she was sitting there, and Madam Eva had to pull her up to her to see what a big girl she was getting. "Isn't like you, is she, to look at? Nor like 'im either. I don't know who she is like, unless it was your Mum, poor soul."

"Is that my Granny?"

"There, poor little darling, bless her little heart, losing her Granny and her only eight-year-old."

Janet wasn't shy, and she was taught to speak nice to people. "Did you know my Granny?" she asked Madam Eva.

Jean was going to stop her, but she hadn't got time.

"Granny came here the other night; she came the night she went away."

"Did she? Did your Mummy see 'er then?"

"Janet, lovey..."

"Mum was asleep. *I* saw her, though."

Madam Eva stared. She pulled Janet round and gave her a hard stare.

"Lovey, run and see for Mum if the kettle's boiling in the kitchen."

Madam Eva turned round on Jean. "And you never told me that. Well, you are lucky with 'er, aren't you? I expect Norman's pleased, isn't 'e?"

Jean jumped up and pushed the door shut after Janet. "Don't you dare tell him! Don't you dare!"

"What! You don't mean you're keepin' it from 'im?"

Jean was listening for Janet coming back. "He hasn't got to know," she said, quick and low. "I'm not having any of that for her. I won't have it, see?"

"Oh, well. Well, I never." Madam Eva was getting quite huffy. "If she's got it in 'er, though, you can't stop 'er."

"Don't you ever dare to let him know."

"*I'm* not going to tell 'im. Don't you go on at *me*. If you ask me you're 'alf balmy, with a good thing like that fallen in your lap and won't do anything with it."

"Never mind what I am. You let her alone."

"I'll let 'er alone all right. Don't you go on so."

Jean heard Janet coming and opened the door.

"Is it ready, lovey? Then you come and help Mum put out the cups."

She wasn't going to leave her there alone with Madam Eva.

"What're you going to do with 'er, then, when she's grown?" Madam Eva always got her good temper back over her cup of tea.

"She'll go in for being a teacher, or for nursing—something nice and refined. Won't you, lovey?"

"My, you have got ideas for 'er!"

"And you mind," Jean told her when she was going. "Don't you dare"

"Don't you fret yourself. I don't see 'im once in a blue moon."

Jean told Janet, "Lovey, never say again to anyone about seeing Granny, will you? You just remember what I told you when you were a little thing. Never say to anyone about seeing things or people."

"Why not, Mum? Is it a secret about Granny?"

"It's a thing you never ought to talk about, whether it's Granny or anyone else. It's all right so long as you keep it to yourself, but don't ever say it."

"I won't ever say it except to you, Mum."

It gave Jean cold shivers to think if Norman had been at home. But he was away a long time this time. When he did come back the funeral was all over long ago, and Janet had forgotten about her Granny.

Then he started taking notice of' Janet, as he never had before, now she was growing up. And more so as she got bigger—wanting her to come and sit on his knee. But she wouldn't; she was frightened of him. Then he put on his soft voice for her—it was a long time since Jean heard that—and started calling her, "My dear little girl."

It would be sometimes after tea, when he was sitting in the kitchen and she'd be playing by herself or reading a storybook over in a corner. Leo was never there playing with her; he always ran out again as soon as he'd had his tea. And Norman would start calling to her, "Come here, my dear little girl."

And she'd stand up and look at him, for all the world like a rabbit looking at a snake, scared to death. And he'd tell her, "Come along"; and when she got over there he'd just smile at her and pat his knee until she had to do what he wanted and sit on it.

"Pretty little girl," he'd say. "Are you fond of your old Dad?"

He liked to get her playing with his watch-chain, and she would sometimes; he had a lot of charms hanging jingling on it. And then he'd stroke her hair and smile at her and tell her it was bedtime for little girls, and try to make her put her head down on his shoulder and go to sleep.

Janet wouldn't, though; she was all strained and taut. And Jean didn't know what to do sometimes, knowing how she was scared of him. She had to tell herself, After all, why shouldn't he hold her if he wants to?

Once he picked up Janet's hand and started reading it, and Jean was on thorns he'd say something. But he only smiled to himself.

Janet would begin to wriggle. "Can I get down and 'elp Mum wash up?"

"Mum, Mum. It's always Mum."

But he'd let her go, and then he'd sit with his usual look on, until Leo came swaggering in, defiant, late as usual.

As likely as not Norman would get up and give him a clip over the ear. "That's a nice time to come home, at your age." Then he'd sit down again and call him over: "Come here."

Leo would come and stand in front of him, sulky-looking, until Norman put his smile on again. "Well, my boy, aren't *you* fond of your old Dad?"

Then he'd brighten up, glib and hopeful. "Yes, Dad!"

And Norman would tell him, "That's right; here's a shilling for you."

But if he was in one of his worst moods he'd give him another clout and say, "Take that for telling lies!"

He'd go off for weeks at a time, and then turn up suddenly and expect them to be all over him.

Jean could breathe freer when he was away. If he was about she'd be worrying all the time while she was seeing a client, wondering if he was back yet, and whether it was time for the school to be out, and why Janet was so scared of him; he'd never done anything to her.

She had enough to keep her wondering, even when he wasn't there—wondering when he'd come back sudden, and if Janet was still seeing things like she used to, and if she ever said it to the girls at school, and if Norman would ever find out. She didn't like to ask Janet if she did, for fear of putting it into her head.

And if it wasn't Janet it was Leo, who was getting so rough, running with a lot of rough boys, and no one could do anything with him; he wouldn't listen to anything she said. And Norman never there; and he wasn't any good when he was.

She'd run over the lines of a hand. "You've had a lot of worries," she'd say.

And the client would mutter, "Oo, yes, I have!" Janet might grow out of it. A lot of children see things, they don't go on when they're grown up.

"There's a son or daughter of yours that's worrying you."

"Oo, that would be my Bill."

The worst was they were both getting big now. And suppose Norman starts on about what she'll do when she leaves school.... If he started on asking her.... I'll have to warn her not to say anything.

"You mustn't worry," she said. She always told them that. "Worry never did anything. You'll find it will all come right if you wait and hope."

She always knew something would happen about Leo. And one afternoon when Norman was out there was a letter for him from the school. She knew it was something had; she had a feeling she ought to open it and not leave it for him. It was for him to go and see the headmaster, and he wouldn't be in till school was over, so she went herself.

When she got back there was only Janet in. "Where's Leo?" she asked her. "Where's Dad? Hasn't he come in yet?"

"Why, Mum, whatever is the matter? You're as white as a sheet."

"Never you mind," she told her. "It's Leo; he's been a bad boy."

She was ever so worried. Whatever was going to happen to him if he went on like that. "Where's Dad? I've got to see him the minute he comes in."

She heard him then and went out to tell him before he could interrupt her: "Norman, Leo's been ever such a bad boy. They sent round from the school. You've got to talk to him when he comes in."

Norman walked on in, looking at her in his usual way. "What's the fuss now? Can't you leave the boy alone?"

"He's a thief," she said, panting, keeping up with him. "He's been stealing—stealing money from a boy at school, and telling lies about it."

"Stealing, eh? All right, I'll talk to him."

"And telling lies too," she said. "You've got to be firm with him, Norman."

Leo didn't come in at tea-time, and when he did he walked in with his usual swagger, but not quite so sure of himself; he didn't know if they'd heard anything from the school.

Norman got up and shouted at him, "Come here! Here," he told him, "honesty's the best policy. Don't you know that yet, at your age?"

Leo went stubborn. He knew then it had come out.

"Honesty's the best policy," Norman told him. "Put that in your head and keep it there. Where do you think you'll get if you go on like that? Do you want to find yourself in gaol?"

Leo only looked at him stubborn; the way he always did when Norman shouted.

"Well, you remember that," Norman told him, going to sit down again.

"Norman," Jean said faintly; she could see Leo didn't care. "Norman, he can't grow up a thief."

"Ah," said Norman, giving her a sneer, "I forgot that." He started taking his belt off. "Come here," he told Leo. "Your Mum thinks you can't remember without something to help you." He let out at him suddenly with the belt, and Leo set up a howl, he was so surprised.

Norman lost his temper then. He might have only meant to give him one, but when Leo let out a howl he took hold of him and went at him till he was out of breath, and Jean was standing there with her hands to her mouth, she didn't know what to say to stop him. "Jan-it, lovey," she remembered, "run and stay in the other room. Do, lovey, do—to please Mum."

When Norman was out of breath he stopped, but he still had the breath left to sneer at her. "You can thank your Mum for that," he told Leo.

Just did it to set him against her.

Leo ran out of the house, and he didn't come back that night.

Janet was so upset that Jean couldn't get her to go to sleep. She stayed up with her in the kitchen after Norman had gone to bed, waiting for her to drop off and Leo to come home. But Janet kept saying she could still see Dad there going on at Leo, and she didn't want to be left.

When she did drop off at last and Leo still hadn't come in Jean put the door on the latch for him and went to bed. But she couldn't sleep. She kept going over it, and what was going to happen to them all—Leo telling lies, and Janet getting upset the way she did over everything. Suppose Leo didn't come back, suppose he ran off and got into bad ways, worse than ever. He was due to leave school now in a few months, and whatever were they going to do with him—especially if he didn't turn out any better than he was now. And Norman setting him against her like that....

It was starting to get light when she thought, He ought to go in Ted's garage; Ted ought to give him a job.

She hadn't seen Ted for years, except at Mum's funeral, but he couldn't refuse to do something for Leo, his own flesh and blood. That's what he'll have to do. It's about the sort of job he could be trained to; he's big and strong.

Leo came in for breakfast before Norman was up. She didn't say any more to him; she only gave him his food. She knew he hated her from the way he looked at her. He went out after, but she didn't ask him whether he was going to school.

She saw Janet off, and then Norman. Norman took his case with him, so he wouldn't be back for a day or two. As she watched him go off from the front window, with his rolled-up umbrella and his brushed suit, she suddenly thought, He's afraid Leo might turn against him. He's afraid of him—that's why he's going.

She dusted up the sitting-room, ready, and tidied herself in case anyone should come. But she felt like death; she did hope no one would.

Only one did, and she wanted trance, but Jean wouldn't do it for her.

"I'm ever so sorry, I'm not very well, and I shouldn't like to disappoint you."

"Oh, dear! I'll make an appointment then, can I? For another day?"

"I'm ever so sorry; I'm not taking anyone for trance anymore."

She didn't know what came over her to say that, but she wasn't sorry. "I'll read the cards for you, though, if you like," she said quickly. She couldn't afford to let her go altogether.

She laid them out, though she couldn't stop her hands shaking, and read off the meanings. She could have done it in her sleep almost by now.

School wouldn't be out for another half-hour and she'd be free by then. Suppose Leo started getting nasty to Janet if she wasn't there? He wouldn't, though, he isn't a bad boy, he's only high-spirited. I ought to tell Norman about putting him with Ted.

Janet still had another two years at school, or more if she was going in the teaching or nursing. Only he might get on to her at any time about it; I ought to warn her.

She thought again next day, I reely must warn Janet before Norman comes back this time.

"Lovey," she asked her that night when they were sitting alone, "suppose Dad asked you if you ever saw anything—you know, when you were little, or about Gran that time—you'd say no, wouldn't you, duck?"

Janet looked at her with her big, solemn eyes. "Oo, Mum, but I couldn't say no when it isn't true, could I?"

Jean didn't know how to answer that. "But, lovey," she said, begging her almost, "you don't ever see things now, do you?"

"Sometimes, Mum. It's ever so funny. Mum, you know when Dad hit Leo the other day?"

"Yes, my duck."

"Well, I saw it happen ever so long ago. Once when Dad was here in the kitchen, and Leo, I saw Dad get up and hit 'im, and keep on doing it, like he did, you know—only he didn't; he never touched 'im. And then when he did it was the very same I saw.

What is it, Mum?"

"It's the Sight," she said. She was coming over faint; she shook it off. She thought at the same time, So that's why she was frightened of him; it was only that. "It's only that some can see things that haven't happened yet—that others can't see. Was there ever anything else?" she made herself ask.

"Not like that, Mum—not reely. Only... Only I did think p'raps he might hurt you some time."

"What, Dad? No, he won't ever hurt me, my duck."

"Oo, Mum, I don't know; I did see it   "

"Only listen, lovey: if he should ever ask you if you saw anything you say no. It'll only harm you if you don't."

"But, Mum, I can't say it if it isn't true?"

"Truth's a funny thing, duck. You can't hardly say sometimes.... But about that, you say no, lovey; you say it just to please Mum."

It was a funny thing, the feeling she had about that. For he did start on at Janet—not the next time he came home, but a week or two later, when it was a question of what Leo was going to do, leaving school.

They had words about that, Jean saying he ought to go in Ted's garage, and Norman saying he wouldn't have his son a working-man in overalls; he knew someone would give him a job in an office.

"But, Norman, he'd more likely keep straight with a healthy outdoors job."

"Don't be a bloody fool!" Norman told her. "That boy'll make money; he'll make his mark in the world."

And then he started on with Janet: "And what about this one? Come over here," he told her. "Come and talk to your old Dad."

He made her sit on his knee, and then he tipped up her face and stared hard into it. "What about you, my little girl?" he asked her in his soft voice. "You going to do a job like Mum?"

"I don't know." She stared back at him, solemn.

"Born under Saturn," he said. "Aquarius," he said. "You ought to."

"She wants to be a nurse," Jean told him.

"Nobody asked you, did they?"

When he let go of her chin Janet hung her head down.

"You tell your old Dad. Now, did you ever hear any spirits talking to you? Just think. Ever heard or seen anything you didn't understand?"

"No."

"What, you never heard any strange little girl coming talking to you? Don't you see anything when you shut your eyes? You think. Not when you go to bed at nights?"

She hung her head. She was red all down her neck. "No."

Norman looked annoyed; he gave her a shake. "And mind your manners."

"No, Dad."

He tried again, coaxing her. "You mean to tell Dad you never saw anything but what's in front of you?"

"No." She only whispered it; she was red as fire.

And then he got tired of it and pushed her off his knee. "Get out! I can see what it is; you're a chip off the old block."

He left her alone after that, though.

And after Leo had gone away from home to his office job and to live near his work Norman didn't come nearly so much as he used to; Jean had Janet to herself, nearly. After Janet had gone off to school in the mornings she did her shopping early, not to miss clients by being out, and tidied the place up and got ready. She usually had two or three in a day, and she didn't let them off so easy now. "You'll get better results," she'd tell them, "if you have the lot—hand, cards, and psychology. Seven-and-six that comes to."

Sometimes they wouldn't feel like spending that much, and then she had to coax them to have the two, at least. "Tell you what I'll do," she'd say: "the lot comes to seven-and-six, but I'll do it for you for five shillings." And they'd have it, most times.

Then there'd be enough over, the end of the week, for her to take Janet to the pictures.

But most of all she wanted it for putting by, for Janet later on—when she started out being a nurse. And not only that, but she had to stay on longer at the school than most of them; go on to the secondary, to get her exam before they'd take her at the hospital. And what's more they wouldn't have her till she was going on for eighteen. You'd need a bit behind you, keeping her home all that time.

"It's worth your while, isn't it," she'd say, "having the best reading you can?" And she took a lot of trouble with them too; she didn't rush them through, the way Madam Eva used to sometimes. She liked clients to go away satisfied. And then she'd give them her card. "You come back in six months or a year, and I'll be able to tell you further ahead."

"Oh, yes," they'd say. "I will."

They wouldn't, though, hardly any of them. Most of this sort wouldn't go to the same twice. They'd give the card to someone else, though. It was different with someone like Madam Eva; she had a few old people who'd always been to her. And for trance again, you got regulars for that; people liked the same once they got used to them. But Jean hardly got anyone for trance now, not once in six months. She almost wished she hadn't told that one that time that she wasn't doing it. She couldn't have gone off and told it all round, though. It was only that it was too expensive for them; p'raps if she put it down a bit she could get more to have it.

She saw that one time when she had an elderly lady there—it was generally the elderly ones that wanted it. The lady asked for hand and cards, and Jean got her to have the seven-and-six one, and when she'd told it nearly all for her the lady suddenly said, shy-like, "You can see people that're dead, can't you? Can you see my son for me?"

Jean said, "I can't see him in the cards, can I? But I can bring him to talk to you, if you like. That means me going in a trance."

The lady said, "Oh. Could you? Do you? Only..." She didn't like to ask, quite. "Isn't that very expensive?"

She didn't look very well off, but she wasn't a poor person.

"It's generally ten shillings for trance," Jean told her.

"Oh, dear!"

"But I'll tell you what I'll do. I'll make it seven-and-six, as you've had the other. That's fifteen shillings for the lot. Will that do for you?"

She took it, that one. Sometimes, though, Jean had to bring it down lower still. "Tell you what, then—just for this once I'll do it for you for twelve-and-six the lot."

She got quite a few that way. She was putting by a nice little bit for Janet. She was going to the secondary now, needing more clothes; it all made it harder. And Norman staying away more and more, though that was a blessing in disguise, for if it meant she had to keep the home going on her own it stopped him upsetting Janet, going on at her for not earning yet at her age.

"If I choose to keep her, what's that to you?" Jean asked him once.

And Janet would stand up to him too nowadays. When he told her, "Come and talk to your old Dad," she'd just give him a look, and go on with her lessons she had to do in the kitchen in the evenings, where it was warm. He got tired of it alter a bit and left her alone. And then one time he went off he didn't come back like he usually did.

It was just before Janet passed her exam and left school. She had nearly a year to wait still before they'd take her at the hospital, and she got a job looking after two little girls whose mother was out at business all day, and in the evenings she came home and helped her Mum in the house. It was the bright spot of Jean's day when Janet was coming home. She'd try not to have a client late so she'd be free and have it cosy for her before she came in. But she couldn't always manage it; she couldn't really afford to choke any off.

How she did hate it too, having to haggle with them over the money. It was only the thought of Janet that could bring her to do it. And with most of them it was nothing but money, money, all the time. That was what they mostly wanted to know about—that and their boys—except for those that wanted to talk with their relations that had passed over. There was that about trance—you did know you were really helping someone. But most of those for hand and cards, all they wanted to know was, "When will I get a better job?" "Can you see any money coming to me?" "Won't I ever 'ave more money than I've got now?"

Some would come straight out with it, and some would wrap it up, but she could always tell when it was coming—and every time it brought a sigh out of her. And you couldn't tell them no, either; they minded that more than anything. "You won't ever be very rich," she might tell them, "but you won't ever be in want"— and things like that to satisfy them.

She felt tired out by the end of a day. It was taking more out of her than it used to. Trance did, dreadful sometimes. "I'll try," she had to tell them, "I'll try to get him for you. But if he doesn't want to talk I can't make 'im, can I? If I don't get him I daresay I'll get some other spirit that knows him, that can give you a message from 'im."

She had to say that, because she never knew what Daisy would do for her. She used to say, Daisy do help me, there's a love. Bring along her boy for me, do.

Then she'd sit back and shut her eyes and start off talking, quiet and monotonous, all about the lovely spirit-world. It was a good way that; she ought to have thought of it sooner. And after a minute or two, or it might be more, her voice would fade off away from her and she'd hear Daisy taking over; and then she'd come back and see soon enough if the client wasn't satisfied.

"Did you get your message all right?"

Once one complained it didn't make sense.

"You couldn't have understood it right," Jean told her. "I expect when you come to think it over you'll see what it meant."

But she wouldn't take her money, and the lady said she'd come back another day and see if it came through any better.

And once she had to say she couldn't do it. It was at the end of a day, and she was tired out and listening for Janet to come home; it took her mind off it. She started talking, and she couldn't get off. She had to open her eyes and say, "I'm ever so sorry; I'm afraid your friend isn't able to talk just now." Well, Daisy duck, you did let me down that time.

It didn't worry her so much, though, as it would have done when she was doing the *séances*. It was only one lady, and if she didn't come back there were plenty more about. It was from trying to do it at the end of the day; she ought to put trance in the mornings, and make them book in advance.

She wasn't sorry, except for the money, that it hadn't come off. She was tired enough as it was, and it did take it out of you. She went and made herself a cup of tea, waiting for Janet to come. And then Janet came in and saw to things while her Mum had a rest.

"Oo, Mum, you do look fagged! You must've worked ever so hard."

Janet was such a comfort to her now, more than ever she was. She used to tell her, "You have a rest, Mum. You go and have a nice lay-down." And then she'd fuss around her, making her comfy.

Once she told her, "Oo, Mum, did you know your hair's going grey?"

"And no wonder! With the worry and trouble I've had with all of you."

"Oo, Mum."

"Not with you, though, my duck. I didn't mean with you."

"Mum, Dad hasn't been home a long time now, has he?"

"P'raps he won't come back anymore."

"Oughtn't you to find out where he's gone to?"

"Don't you worry, my duck. He'll turn up again, or else 'e won't."

She didn't want him back now till Janet had got off and started her nursing.

Only when she did go it was ever so empty. It was enough to give you the creeps sometimes—all alone there except for when clients came. But Janet came home to see her Mum in her time off, and Jean was so proud of her she couldn't take her eyes off her. She hadn't really seen how pretty Janet had grown until she got away. She was still a little bit of a thing, like a little fairy. It was ever such hard work, she said, in the hospital—hard, rough work mostly when you started; but she didn't mind. And Jean didn't mind working for her, either, and her long, empty evenings to herself, when it meant Janet being happy.

She was almost glad to see clients now—glad apart from what they paid her, since it meant having someone to talk to for half an hour. She gave them good value for their money; she was always ready to listen to all their troubles, and that was what they came for, mostly—that, and to be told it was all coming right for them in the end.

And then Norman showed up, a month or two after Janet went to the hospital. He came in one afternoon, but you could see he didn't mean to stay.

"I thought you weren't coming back," she told him.

"Good riddance, eh?"

He was seedy-looking—more than he used to be. Down on his luck. He was always so smart at one time.

"And I'll be back again before long," he said, "too."

He had a meal and fetched some things he wanted from the cupboard.

"Got any money?" he asked her.

"No. Only what it takes, keeping up the house."

"Go on. You're doing all right. After all I spent on you."

She had to give him a few shillings she'd taken that morning.

When he'd gone she got out the cards and spread them on the kitchen-table. She didn't often tell it for herself—you oughtn't to; it brought bad luck. She'd only taken to it since she'd been alone so much. And this one wasn't for her; it was for Janet. She had to know how Janet was going to get on.

There was a lot of bad in it too; that was what came of doing it yourself. All right, then, she'd do one for Norman—see what was coming to him.

There was a lot of bad everywhere. They always said you never ought to.

She put the cards away and went to bed. But she couldn't resist it in the long evenings when she'd made herself a cup of tea—laying out just one, to see how things were going. Sometimes it came out better than others.

Norman came back again one dinner-time a couple of weeks later, and wanted more money from her.

"I only got five shillings this morning," she told him. "You can 'ave that if you like."

He took it from her, with a look as if he didn't believe her. "Make yourself pretty comfortable, don't you, all the same?"

He settled himself at the table while she cooked him some dinner and laid out their knives and forks.

"You alone here, then?"

"You know that all right," she told him.

It was Janet's long evening off; she was on thorns he wouldn't get out before she came.

"I may as well come and keep you company," he said.

She didn't say anything.

He went off soon after dinner, when he'd warmed himself by the fire. She was so thankful he'd gone before Janet came that she didn't worry much over whether he was coming back to live. If he did he'd be out most of the time, like he was before.

She fetched out the tin of cakes she'd put aside for Janet and tidied herself to look her best and laid the table for tea, in case she was interrupted later. A client came at four o'clock, but she told her, "I'm ever so sorry, could you come back to-morrow?" And the lady said she would.

She made up the fire and got it all cosy and put the kettle on. "There you are, lovey, then!"

But Janet wasn't quite herself. She could see that at once. She didn't say anything, thinking it would blow over. But Janet couldn't eat her tea, whatever was troubling her, and she couldn't keep it to herself, either, even if she wanted to. She came out with it all of a sudden, "Mum, I can't go on with it."

"What, my duck?"

She knew, though; she knew it then, before ever Janet told her.

"The hospital, Mum. It's awful, reely, you don't know. I can't do it; I'll never be any good at it."

Jean told her she was silly, talking like that. But she knew it wasn't any good; there was something behind it.

"It isn't the work, Mum. I don't mind hard work; I wouldn't mind—it's the people dying. Having to see them die, you'd never believe, Mum—you never would think...."

"Why, lovey, you'll soon get over that. All nurses have to, don't they, sometimes? We've all got to die some time."

"But it isn't that, Mum. None of them sees it the way I did."

Jean coaxed it out of her then. But she knew what it was before she was told. She knew it wasn't any good. Her heart was like lead.

"It was like that, Mum, it was this morning, there was a man was going to die, I never had seen one before. They got the screens up round the way they do, and I had to go inside and help, I never did before. And just when he was going, Mum, just before he went, it was like a dark cloud came over 'im; it seemed to come out of 'im, like, and it got almost solid till it was like his own body, the same shape, and it lay there right on top of him. Only you could see through it, if you see what I mean. 'Oo,' I said to the nurse that was there, 'whatever is it?' But she didn't seem to think it was anything. 'He won't be a minute now,' she said. And then just when he let off the rattle, you know—I always heard of that, but I never heard about the other—the body came right up in the air, away from 'im, and almost solid, and it had such a horrible look on its face, not a bit like him, poor thing—you could see 'im underneath, lying there just staring. Dead by then he must've been. Oo, Mum, and I fainted right away! When I came round the nurse had got 'im laid out, and the other thing wasn't there anymore, and the nurse said to me—she was ever so sweet—'You go and lay down a bit,' she said, 'I won't let on.' But the sister saw me, and she was ever so nasty. 'You won't do much good here,' she said, 'if you can't stand a little thing like that. Just a death,' she said. 'What about when you have to see an operation?' 'Oo, I don't want to!' I said. 'But it wasn't that,' I told her, 'it wasn't just him dying'—but she wouldn't listen. 'You'd better pull yourself together,' she said, 'and see a few to get you used to it.'"

Jean said, "There, lovey, p'raps it won't happen another time. P'raps it only just 'appened that once. I'd try again if I were you." But she didn't believe it herself, what she was saying.

She ought to have thought of it sooner. She'd heard that once before—about how you could see that sort of thing when you were psychic. It was another thing that showed there were spirits, didn't it. That just showed. Only she'd never thought of it about Janet, and to think she'd let her go in for nursing...

"I'll tell you what, though, lovey," she coaxed her, "he must've been a bad man, that one, to look nasty like that. Suppose you had some lovely, good person dying, you'd only see a beautiful spirit going away, wouldn't you now? The sort that's good and kind and comes back helping people."

"Don't the bad ones ever come back, Mum?"

"I don't know, my duck. I never heard one. I expect they just go and enjoy themselves, selfish, in the lovely spirit-world, and don't trouble what happens to anyone who's left."

Janet said, "I can't do it, though, Mum."

"I know, my duck."

Jean was worried; she didn't see whatever else Janet could do. It was too late now for her to train for a teacher.

"Unless you go for a children's nurse again—get a regular place. How'd you like that, lovey?"

"That wants training too, Mum. You don't get much of a job if you aren't trained. And you have to pay for the training too."

Jean hadn't the heart to tell her, though, that she must go on where she was. The only thing she could say was she must try to stick it for a bit while they saw about the training. And then she'd scrape it out somehow.

Janet thanked her ever so much, and then she had to run, to be in by ten. When she'd gone Jean sat down and thought it out; she didn't see how she was ever going to do it. She'd have to advertise more, or move to a better district, in a busy street—only then the rent did you in.

She was still thinking it round when Norman came.

He'd got his case with him. It had gone right out of her head that he'd said he was coming home to stop.

She couldn't very well tell him no, even though he hadn't given her a penny for the house for two years at the very least. She hoped anyhow he'd do his share if he was living there, so she could put by a bit more.

But it didn't seem as if he was earning very much. He only went off now in the middle of the morning, saying business was slack up his way. And often when he came in at night she could tell he'd been drinking.

"What about your keep?" she asked him when it came to Saturday.

"You go on, you're doing all right."

She never told him a word about Janet.

She had to try to turn in all she could when he was out.

Will you have the seven-and-six?" she'd say, straight away; or if they were well-off: "I'll throw it all in for ten shillings, for this once."

Then she'd lay out the cards for them, but she'd hardly be hearing what she said herself.

Suppose they made her see another one, another dying.... You never know how it might take her. She was always such a sensitive little t ling. Suppose they made her go seeing something nasty....

"I can see a lot of luck coming to you—a lot of luck. Only you'll 'ave to wait a bit."

Why can't he do his correspondence work like he used to? He could turn in a bit over that to help out. It isn't fair him not even paying his keep. If it was anything else wrong with her I could tell him about it, but I can't ever tell him that.

"You'll have a long life, and a lot of luck. Only you take care, the way I tell you."

Then it was Janet's long evening off coming round again, and Jean didn't know what to do. She sent her a line to tell her her Dad was at home, and not on any account to let on she was leaving the hospital. Only you never knew; he might smell a rat.

She said to Norman, "It's Janet's day off; she'll be round here, I expect"—thinking there was a chance he'd stay out if he didn't want to see her. "It's terrible hard work," she told him, "what they have to do. It gets her fagged right out." In case he should think there was something funny with her.

She got the tea ready, hoping and hoping Janet would turn up first so she could have a word with her before he was there. But Janet never came.

He came presently, and had his tea.

"Where's the girl got to, then?" he asked when he'd done.

"She's got kept, I expect."

She did worry, though, thinking what might have happened to her. She never would go and do anything rash?

"She must've got kept," she thought, slipping the teacakes back to keep warm. "They must've had some emergency case come in and kept her."

She cleared the dirty plates away and swept over the cloth and set Janet's place ready for her again at the end of the clean table. I never ought to have left her there; I ought to've had her home straight off that time.

She's got kept, though—that's all it is. I'll hear from her to-morrow. Or else did she stay away because he was here? She never would do that, though, she'd have let me know. Or didn't she get the chance to slip out and post a letter p'raps? Oh, dear, I never ought to have let her go back.

She took up her crochet. But she couldn't settle to anything; she kept looking up and listening. She might pop in just for a minute. If only he'd go out again—any other night he would.

She won't come, though, now. Wouldn't hardly be worth her while....

Then she heard the front door open, and ran out into the passage.

"Oh, Mum," Janet said. Norman moved back his chair in the kitchen and she didn't say any more.

"Hullo, Dad," she said.

Jean sat her down at the table and put her tea in front of her, but she only played with it. She was as white as a sheet.

Norman asked, "Is that all you've got to say?"

"You got kept, didn't you, lovey?"

Jean was fussing round her. She wanted to find out, only she was in a twitter Norman would tumble to something. "The same as before?" she asked her, giving her a look.

Janet only said, "I'm sorry, Mum; I thought you'd worry if I didn't come at all."

She had to go soon after; she had to be in by ten o'clock. "Wasn't worth your while coming," Norman told her. He was sulky she hadn't taken any more notice of him.

And yet he came out to the door when she was going, so Jean couldn't get a word with her alone.

"Come early next time," she told her, and Janet nodded.

"It's all right, Mum; don't get fretting."

Jean watched her go off down the lit road to the tram.

"What you stopping there for," Norman grumbled—"letting the cold into the house."

She came in and shut the door. "The work's too hard for her," she said. "It's too much for 'er."

Norman shrugged his shoulders.

She cleared the table and got ready for bed. I ought to get her away straight off. I ought to get her home here. If only he wasn't home....

P'raps it wasn't that after all, she thought, getting in. P'raps they hadn't made her see anything. It might be something else had upset her.

She was always like that, easy upset. P'raps she was only feeling poorly.

I ought to get her away, though, she thought, before she dropped off at last. I ought to put her to start the training.

She felt worn out the next morning with the worry of it. And clients kept coming one after the other; she didn't dare refuse them.

"I see a long life in your hand—a long life and a lot of luck."

If only he hadn't been there I would have found out what it was. It would have done her good to talk it over, too.

"Will I get any money coming to me soon?" She sighed as she passed the cards over. "Wish while you shuffle, and cut with the left hand."

I'm as bad, though, having to think all the time how much I can get them to part with.

"You'll get your wish all right. You'll 'ave to wait for it, though."

If only I could get her away from there, if I could get enough together for her to start the training.

"Two-and-six change; that's right, thank you. I'll just give you my card. If you should know of anyone...."

When she was alone for a minute she stood and stretched herself and looked out of the window. The grass was grey and soggy and the path wanted sweeping down. I'll get her away from there whatever happens. She can stay home here till I can manage the training.

Only eleven-thirty, and she'd had three already, and here was another coming in at the gate. What's the matter with them to-day?

She went to the door, tidying her hair, and let the lady in. She could hardly stop a yawn while she asked her what she'd have.

"I'd like my hand read, I think?" She looked as if she didn't even know her own mind.

"You get better results if you have the cards as well," Jean told her, quite sharp; she was out of patience to-day. Rich-looking. Her crocodile bag cost a nice penny. "And psychology. That's ten shillings the lot." Youngish. No; not very, though.

"All right, yes. Well, I'll have the lot then."

Common voice—rich, but common. Wonder if the black's mourning?

She held out her podgy hand, and then she half drew it back. "What I really want—what I wondered... My little boy died a few months back; I do wonder if you couldn't get him for me?"

So it is mourning.

"Well, I'd have to go into a trance for that."

And just when I'm fagged out.... If only I could make a bit, though....

"I'd have to charge you a guinea extra for trance." I can always take it off again. "I'm ever so sorry, but it does take it out of you so. I'll tell you what I'll do, though: I'll do you the lot, *with* trance, for twenty-seven-and-six."

The lady only thought a minute, and then she said yes. It quite took Jean's, breath away.

And just to think of getting a chance like that at the end of a hard morning... Daisy duck, you will help me though, won't you.

She started laying out the cards. You will, won't you, Daisy. Daisy love, I haven't ever needed it so much.

"I can see a lot of trouble you've been through."

It's her little boy she wants to talk to, duck. You'll bring him, won't you, you make him come.

"A big sorrow only a few months back. That would be your little boy."

"Oh, my little Teddy!" said the lady. "And it was so sudden, too."

"Yes, I can see it was. And he was such a bright, cheery little chap, wasn't he? I can see how you've missed him...."

"Only four years old. And he just left go of my hand, and the car came along...."

"Yes, on a road, wasn't it? On a long road with a corner?"

"Yes, that's right. We'd got past the corner, though—we were well round the bend. And he just left go: 'Mammy,' he said, and then the car came around so fast...."

"Oh, dear! Yes, I can see how hard it's been for you. Now I'll tell you what I'll do; I'll go into a trance straight away and ask my spirit-guide to bring him to talk to you, shall I?"

"Oh, thank you ever so!"

Daisy duck, you must, you've got to bring him. He's called Teddy, mind; he's a little boy wants his Mammy. Go on, Daisy duck, you will, won't you.

She settled herself down and shut her eyes. If I can't get off.... Oh my God, I've got to. Daisy duck, you've *got* to do it.

She started off talking in the slow, monotonous voice that sent her off: "I see the lovely world of spirits. It is all around us here. All around with us here to-day....."

Daisy, now, you must. Do be quick, go on.

"Lovely spirits. I see them all around, helping us, waiting to bring us comfort from the world of light...."

Oh God, Daisy, you can't, you can't let me down now, go on, do. He's Teddy. You know. He's a little boy, four years old....

"I see them coming round...."

It wasn't though. It wasn't any good. Her voice was going on; it wasn't going away off. Her eyes were pricking with holding them shut so tight. She was all screwed up, tense; she could have screamed.

It wasn't any good. She couldn't do it. It was from being too tired. You can't miss this one though, you can't, you...

"All the lovely spirits." And then suddenly, out loud, "Mammy! This is Teddy!"

When she'd said it she stopped. She caught in her breath. I can't, I can't do that. I don't care —I've got to, I can't help it.

"Teddy! My little Teddy! Tell Mammy..."

She didn't know. I got the voice all right. How did I.

"Oo, Mammy, it's lovely, it's all lovely flowers and little birdies, it's ever so lovely, Mammy."

"Oh, Teddy-boy, tell Mammy, did it hurt, my precious? How did it feel when it happened?"

"Oo no, Mammy, it didn't hurt, it was just the big car came..."

"Oo-o-o..."

"And then it was all lovely spirit-world and little birdies singing, and toys and things....."

Silly old hen, why does she take it, why does she make me....

"Oh, T-Teddy, do you remember the r-rabbits?"

"Oo, Mammy, yes—all the little bunnies!"

"My own little Teddy!"

God, that'll do, won't that do....

She opened her eyes. The lady was sitting there crying, clasping her hands together, looking as if she was in church.

"He's gone," Jean said, and the lady jumped. "They can't stay for long."

The lady began to wipe her eyes.

She felt turned to stone. "But I expect he'd come another

day," she said stonily.

The lady stuffed her handkerchief away and felt in her bag. "Twenty-seven-and-six you said; I haven't got the change. Never mind, you take the thirty shillings; I'm sure it's worth it. I'm sure I'm ever so grateful to you. I never expected anything so lovely. You'll do it for me again, won't you, another day?"

The door shut behind her and Jean went back to the window. She was as cold as stone. What did she go telling me all that for? It was her fault. She made me do it.

The lady was just going out of the gate, waddling a bit on her high heels, with her fat crocodile bag swinging. The strap caught on the latch and she fumbled it off. She got outside, and her hat went away along the next-door hedge.

Yes and I will, I'll do it again. Yes I will. If I can get a few like her...

She felt cold as death and turned to stone.

Silly old hen, she thought in cold fury, she *liked* it like that.

She turned away from the window. I ought to get the dinner, in case he should come in.

The two notes were lying on the table; she stuffed them down inside her blouse.

The bell rang. Go to hell, she thought. She went to the door, mechanically patting her hair tidy, flat to her head.

"Madam Jean?"

"Come in," she told her.

Young. Working. Must've come out of work at twelve.

She sat her at the table and gathered up the cards and knocked them into a pack. "Now what would you like? Hand? Cards? You can have hand, cards, 'n' psychology, ten shillings."

"Oo, I don't think I—"

"Well, I'll tell you what I'll do, just for this once—I'll do you the lot for seven-and-six."

Afterword
by Rebecca Bowler

Trance By Appointment (1939) was Gertrude Trevelyan's final novel. It is a sparely written and claustrophobic narrative in which Jean, a young working-class girl, finds herself blessed—or cursed—with psychic abilities. Inevitably, when people find out, her gifts are in demand. A childhood friend insists that she read her palm—"Oh go on do, you know you can, can't you Jean, do look at my 'and for me, do, go on"[1]—despite Jean's protests that she doesn't know how. As a teenager she finds herself unable to hold down a job at a kiosk because she empathically shares all the stresses and the pain of the commuters who pass her every day. She becomes apprenticed to a medium called Madam Eva who quickly realises that Jean can go into a trance—"She's got it! Didn't I tell you she's got it!"[2]—and immediately tells her friend Mr Mitch, the astrologer, who decides that Jean is a commodity. He decides to marry her and set her up in a house

1   G.E. Treveylan, *Trance By Appointment*, p.26.

2   Ibid., p.69.

so that she can exercise her abilities for his profit. She is suddenly subject to a timetable and must fall into trances, and summon her guide, by appointment. The story is one of demand after demand. Jean is coerced into the role of fortune-teller. She is never allowed to develop as an individual but is continually cast as "medium"—a conduit rather than a woman: for the spirits to talk through; for her Mr Mitch's financial dreams; for the emotional soothing of her clients.

Trevelyan's style owes a great debt to the novels-of-consciousness which were prevalent from the late 1910s into the 1930s. The novel, from the very first pages, gives us access to Jean's consciousness through a free indirect style which blends authorial third person with the simple language Jean might use to speak to herself. When Jean is a child, her perceptions are muddled. She sees—"there was a paper running along the pavement"—and she hears—"it went flap-flap and ran along and stopped." She feels her own body's movements, in her seat on the mailcart, as a series of bumps, and she watches the "boy on a bicycle," himself bumping along the pavement.[3] There is no sense of cause and effect and no higher-level reasoning here. There is just the perceiving self, receiving a series of sensations: vision, sound, and bodily feeling. This is modernist experiment similar to Virginia Woolf's lauded representation of childhood consciousness in her 1931 novel *The Waves*:

> "I see a ring," said Bernard, "hanging above me. It quivers and hangs in a loop of light."
>
> "I see a slab of pale yellow," said Susan, "spreading away until it meets a purple stripe."
>
> "I hear a sound," said Rhoda, "cheep, chirp; cheep, chirp; going up and down."[4]

---

3   Ibid., p.13.

4   Virginia Woolf, *The Waves* (Oxford: Oxford University Press, 1992), p.3.

It is similar, too, to the young Mary Olivier's sensations at the beginning of the novel of the same name by May Sinclair: "The big white globes hung in a ring above the dinner table. At first, when she came into the room, carried high in Jenny's arms, she could see nothing but the hanging, shining globes."[5] In each the child perceives the world innocently and without association: the paper is just paper, the bumps are just bumps; the rings and globes are not curtain rings or lightshades, they are just rings and globes; the paper and its flapping are everything. As Jean gets older, her perceptions become more complicated. She sees, and she questions what she sees; she reflects and worries. She is though, all the way to the end, a simple woman. Her consciousness never has the chance to develop beyond its use-value to the people around her.

When the child Jean is sitting in her mailcart, noticing the paper blowing down the street and the boy on the bicycle, gurgling and looking and listening, she next sees a series of "bubbles." It's unclear at first what these are. Jean, at this point, does not have a consciousness equipped to see them as anything more than just further examples of the myriad visual impressions that come when you are outside in the big, bright world: "there was a big blue bubble and it burst, and another, and white ones too, big and shiny, and Jean gurgled and grabbed at them, but they went away and then there were more."[6] These bubbles, it turns out, are not really there. Later, when she is halfway between waking and sleeping, she sees the bubbles again, only this time they contain pictures: "There was a big river with little boats on, like the canal where Tom went fishing tiddlers, and trees all along instead of houses."[7]

---

5   May Sinclair, *Mary Olivier: A Life* (London: Cassell, 1919), p.4.

6   *Trance By Appointment*, p.13.

7   Ibid, p.14.

These visions seem, to Jean, entirely natural. It is only when she asks her parents what the images are and why they come, that she begins to become aware that there is something unusual in the fact she can see them. "Stuff and nonsense," says her mother. "Don't tell lies," says her father. But the next time her Auntie Lil visits, her mother, thinking that Jean is not listening, tells a different story: "It's the second sight."[8] This is the first clue Jean has that she is different, and crucially, as soon as she realises this, she is caught in a contradictory cycle of recognition and denial, fear and secrecy. The central tension of Jean's lifelong narrative is set up in these first few pages: the gift is real, but it is secret; it is authentic, but it is suspect. Her mother is distrustful, in particular, of commercial fortune-telling, which, in her mind, is *not* authentic. As she says to Auntie Lil: "I don't hold with that, as you very well know. That's all lies. Those that 'ave the Sight keep it to themselves."[9]

The novel never quite resolves to what extent Jean's gift is real. We could read the trances at face value, as communication with the spirit world; we could read them as psychological states not yet explained by science. The *Times* reviewer read the novel as the story of "an ingenuous and untutored mind, and the girl's transition from a half-fearful, half-grateful acceptance of her gift to doubt of its genuineness", which transition "is made slowly and subtly."[10] This reviewer takes as read that Jean's disillusionment with her abilities is rational doubt; a waking up to reality. The narrative is a little more complicated than that, however. One stage-post on the road to disillusionment is when she realises her spirit guide, Daisy, never existed; Mr Mitch has made up that he had a sister

---

8   Ibid., p.16.

9   Ibid., p.17.

10   Anonymous, 'New Novels: The Fortune-Teller', *The Times*, Friday September 15, 1939.

called Daisy. She is distraught, but even in her distress she holds on to the certainty that *something* is talking through her:

> Jean wiped her eyes. "Daisy's lies—then it's all lies. There aren't any spirits. Then what is it that talks?"
>
> "What! How the devil do *I* know? You ought to know—you've done it long enough."[11]

Then, later:

> "Mum says it's only yourself. It's only that when you go off you know things you don't when you're all there."
>
> Madam Eva got quite annoyed over that. "'Ow does *she* know? *She* isn't clairvoyante, is she?"[12]

Jean could be, she thinks, channelling real spirits, if not Daisy. On the other hand, she could be tuning into some aspect of her non-conscious mind, which would explain why she can't remember what she had said while in trance.

It's possible that Trevelyan had read some of the ongoing research into psychical phenomena undertaken by the Society for Psychical Research, in whose journal the validity of psychic phenomena was debated in precisely these terms. Founded in 1882, the Society is still active today. May Sinclair, that other mystic modernist, was a member; Arthur Conan Doyle was too, although he resigned in 1930 in protest at what he saw as "unscientific" cynicism in the Society's research methods.[13] Its presidents

---

11   *Trance by Appointment.*, p.149.

12   Ibid., p.152.

13   Elizabeth Savage, 'Challenging Challenger: The Fallout Between Arthur Conan Doyle and the Society for Psychical Research', *Cambridge Special Collections blogpost* [https://specialcollections-blog.lib.cam.ac.uk/?p=17548#_ftn5].

were variously philosophers, mathematicians, psychologists, politicians and lawyers, and it tried to maintain a scientific attitude to its research, albeit not strictly the physicalist attitude that scientists today would favour. Key to the Society's research were observations of séances and the society had its own séance room, which could be booked for scientific observation. The 1937-8 volume of the *Journal of the Society for Psychical Research* publishes reports of several experiments with different mediums, performed under "rigid conditions of experimental control."[14] The Society's research also drew extensively on psychoanalysis, particularly the work of Carl Jung and the journal published debates, begun in the lecture hall and carried through "reports" and the letter pages of the journal, as to which parts of the mind—unconscious, subconscious, superconscious—are involved in trance mediumship, and whether the mind is more awake or more asleep when in trance.

Edith Lyttelton (née Balfour), the novelist and playwright, was the president of the Society for Psychical Research in 1933 and 1934. Her 1931 book, *Our Superconscious Mind*, constitutes one of the many attempts in the early twentieth century to apply psychological and psychoanalytic principles to the study of psychic phenomena and to begin to theorise its probable causes. She reaches rather further than Jung, however, and posits a "superconsciousness"—a more mystical concept even than Jung's collective unconscious. The "superconscious" is the part of the mind which, in Lyttelton's words, "is already inhabiting another field of existence." It can connect with the past and the future, and across space; it is not confined to the knowledge of the individual's consciousness,

---

14   *Journal for the Society for Psychical Research* Vol. XXX (1937-8). Tavistock Square, London, p.56.

subconsciousness, or even unconsciousness.[15] "A medium", Lyttelton says, "will tap the knowledge of his or her superconscious mind and express it, often very haltingly and inadequately."[16] Some of the "flashes" produced will be true and can be evidenced, but the medium cannot be sure how he or she came by them.

Trevelyan responds to this debate with *Trance By Appointment*, but she doesn't attempt to give a definitive answer as to what the visions are and how they come. The trance really happens and the voice really speaks through Jean; what or *who* speaks is variously certain and uncertain. The unwitting Jean, whose connexion to the "spirit-world" is not one she understands and who remembers nothing of her trances after the fact, still believes in the "gift" itself at the end of the novel. She is anxious about her daughter Janet's empathic fatigue and hides the fact that Janet is now seeing visions. Janet, now a nurse, is coming home from work spiritually exhausted in a similar way to the young Jean. She sees a spirit rise from the body of a dying man and as she tells this to her mother, Jean reflects: "She ought to have thought of it sooner. She'd heard that once before—about how you could see that sort of thing when you were psychic. It was another thing that showed there were spirits, didn't it. That just showed."[17]

Jean does not then become disillusioned with her gift. Her ultimate defeat is instead in what the Times reviewer called "the struggle against fraud."[18] When she first picked up the crystal ball, ready to learn, Madam Eva told her:

---

15   Edith Lyttelton, *Our Superconscious Mind* (London: Philip Allan, 1931), p.269.

16   Ibid., p.242.

17   *Trance By Appointment*, p.183.

18   Anonymous, 'New Novels: The Fortune-Teller', *The Times*, Friday September 15, 1939.

There's a lot can be learnt from faces. Now when you got 'er holding it you take a good look at 'er—don't look too much as if you're looking, mind—and sum 'er up in your own mind. How old is she, and what money's she got? You'll have to sum that up quick when you got clients regular. Remember this, though—every one wants money, it doesn't matter how much they got. That's always a safe one.[19]

This is a game of psychology, not one of "connexion" to the spirit-world.[20] At first this is presented as what Jean should do when the "connexion" fails to work; as time goes on it becomes the main game. While Jean feels that she is helping people and giving them comfort, she is also aware that she is mainly telling them what they want to hear—which is mostly about monetary and emotional needs. People want to hear that they will make money, make a good marriage, and live a prosperous life; they want to hear that their passed-on relatives are happy, that there is an afterlife, and there is hope for solace after death. They want hope in the immediate messiness of life or they want ultimate hope for something more after. Towards the end of the novel, Jean begins to feel that what she is giving people is not comfort anymore:

And with most of them it was nothing but money, money, all the time. That was what they mostly wanted to know about—that and their boys—except for those that wanted to talk with their relations that had passed over. There was that about trance—you did know you were really helping some one. But most of those for hand and cards, all they wanted to know was, "When will I get a better job?" "Can you see any money coming to me?" "Won't I ever 'ave more money than I've got now?"[21]

---

19   *Trance By Appointment*, p.49.

20   Ibid., p.109.

21   Ibid., p.196.

Although Trevelyan herself came from a well-to-do family, she is adept at portraying the proliferating and wearying demands of working-class life. Her novel of the previous year, *Theme With Variations* (1938), also features a cast of characters who begin with noble ideals and who are pulled and pushed and harried by circumstance until their lives become a series of compromises. The gradual erosion of Jean's principles is her change of practice from mostly trance—which might really help people—to mostly cards and hands—which constitutes, in her own reckoning, exploitation of people's economic anxiety. Jean knows what it is to be poor and she did not mind when she was taking money from people she considered "rich people."[22]

At the end of the novel, Jean has two experiences which signal that she has fallen. In the first, she fakes a trance, telling her rich client what she wants to hear. In the second, she realises her client is poor but sells her the full package anyway. The fall then happens in two stages. In the first, she becomes a fraud, *performing* a trance in lieu of real mediumship. In the second, she betrays her own working-class community: she sells false solace to people who can't really afford to buy it. Her tragedy, then, is that she compromises her ideals and moves closer and closer to the attitude of the anonymous fortune-tellers whose vignettes punctuate the book: "It takes a lot of seein', this does. Now, come along, dear, I c'n 'elp you, reely I can. I c'n see big things comin' for yer, only jus' round the corner."[23]

In her portrayal of ordinary lives, Trevelyan is part of an emerging movement in the 1930s towards unflinching narratives of ordinary lives and everyday hardships. Critics often credit Walter

---

22   Ibid., p.155.

23   Ibid., p.168.

Greenwood's *Love on the Dole* (1933) as an early and pioneering example of this impulse. Its style was distinctly literary and indebted to literary modernism, but it was also written, in large part, in dialect. It combined the highbrow and intertextual with "distinctively working-class tone and content." As Jack Windle points out, Greenwood's novel began a tradition of working-class writing which flourished into the 1950s and 1960s. It showed how working-class lives could be presented in their full complexity: "without the strict division between Standard English narration and dialogue in the demotic register [...] laying claim to the novel as a form fit for the expression of working-class experience."[24]

Trevelyan was an early practitioner of this democratising movement in literature. Her novels are literary and they are demotic: Jean's simple voice colouring the narrative of the whole, for example. They show the real aching tragedy of an ordinary working-class life, with its privations, compromises and worries, and they do so without condescending. Trevelyan's final novel feels like a transitional novel between the inner-gaze of the modernists and the documentary scrutiny of everyday life beginning to develop in the 1930s. Perhaps this is one reason she has been so thoroughly forgotten: we are never sure what to make of writers who have one foot in one movement and one in another. If anything, though, her status as late-modernist-naturalist signals her importance. She was at the forefront of what was to be a important movement in literature: the social realism of the mid-century.

---

24   Jack Windle, '"What life means to those at the bottom": *Love on the Dole* and its Reception since the 1930s', Literature and History 20, no. 2 (October 2011), p.46.

Gertrude Eileen Trevelyan was born in Bath in 1903. She came to fame as the first woman to win the Newdigate Prize for best undergraduate poem at Oxford. Starting with *Appius and Virginia* in 1932, she published eight novels, her last being *Trance by Appointment* in 1939. Her novels *Two Thousand Million Man-Power*, *William's Wife*, and *As It Was in the Beginning* have been reissued in the Recovered Books series from Boiler House Press. Injured when a German bomb struck her flat in October 1940, she died at her parents' home in March 1941.

Louisa Treger is the author of four acclaimed novels: *The Lodger* (2014), *The Dragon Lady* (2019), *Madwoman* (2022), and *The Paris Muse* (2024). She has written for *The Times*, *The Telegraph*, *Tatler*, *BBC History Magazine*, and *English Heritage*. She has a First Class degree and a PhD in English literature from University College London.

Rebecca Bowler is Senior Lecturer in Twentieth Century English Literature at Keele University. She is the author of *Literary Impressionism: Vision and Memory in Dorothy Richardson, Ford Madox Ford, H.D. and May Sinclair* (Bloomsbury, 2016) and is writing a book on nutritional science, eating, and fitness narratives in the early twentieth century, provisionally titled *Modernist Wellness*. She is co-General Editor on the forthcoming *Edinburgh Critical Editions of the Works of May Sinclair* and is preparing *Mary Olivier: A Life, The New Idealism, and Arnold Waterlow: A Life* for publication.

Other Titles in the Recovered Books series from
Boiler House Press

Gentleman Overboard by Herbert Clyde Lewis
Introduction by George Szirtes, Afterword by Brad Bigelow
ISBN: 9781913861230

Pull Devil, Pull Baker by Stella Benson
Introduction by Julia Blackburn, Afterword by Nicola Darwood
ISBN: 9781913861605

Time: the Present – Selected Stories by Tess Slesinger
Introduction by Vivian Gornick, Afterword by Paula Rabinowitz
ISBN: 9781913861582

Two Thousand Million Man-Power by Gertrude Trevelyan
Introduction by Rachel Hore, Afterword by Brad Bigelow
ISBN: 9781913861858

Quarry by Jane White
Introduction by Anne Billson, Afterword by Helen Hughes
ISBN: 9781915812001

The Sanity Inspectors by Friedrich Deich
Introduction by Sinclair McKay, Afterword by Chris Maloney
ISBN: 9781913861872

To Test the Joy: Selected Poetry and Prose by Genevieve Taggard
Introduction by Terese Svoboda, Edited and with commentary
by Anne Hammond
ISBN: 9781915812025

William's Wife by Gertrude Trevelyan
Introduction by Alice Jolly, Afterword by Anne Kennedy Smith
ISBN: 9781915812063

Time Stood Still by Paul Cohen-Portheim
Introduction by Andrea Pitzer, Afterword by Panikos Panayi
ISBN: 9781915812056

No More Giant by Joaquina Ballard Howles
Introduction by Judy Blunt, Afterword by Nancy Cook
ISBN: 9781915812094

Mortal Leap by MacDonald Harris
Introduction by Jonathan Coe, Afterword by Steven G. Kellman
ISBN: 9781915812100

As It Was in the Beginning by Gertrude Trevelyan
Introduction by Kim Adrian, Afterword by Stanislava Dikova
ISBN: 9781913861582

The Bitter Roots by Norman Macleod
Introduction by Joanna Pocock, Afterword by Gabriella Graceffo
ISBN: 978191915812384

Red House Alley by Else Jerusalem
Introduction by Sophie Haydock, Afterword by Stephanie G. Ortega
Translated by Stephanie G. Ortega
ISBN: 9781915812360

Other Titles in the Recovered Books series from Boiler House Press

Solitary Confinement by Christopher Burney
Introduction by Ted Gioia, Afterword by Hugh Purcell
ISBN: 9781915812469